A PATRIOT'S A TO Z OF AMERICA

★

A PATRIOT'S

A TO Z

OF

AMERICA

THINGS EVERY GOOD
AMERICAN SHOULD KNOW

★

EDWARD P. MOSER

MJF BOOKS
NEW YORK

Published by MJF Books
Fine Communications
322 Eighth Avenue
New York, NY 10001

A Patriot's A to Z of America
LC Control Number: 2015937056
ISBN 978-1-60671-302-0

QF   10 9 8 7 6 5 4 3 2 1

To America's pioneers—of the frontier, the air and sea,
the science lab, the battlefield, social mores,
and the political realm.

CONTENTS

INTRODUCTION

It's a daunting thing, to be asked to write narratives, however brief, on important people, events, and trends in a canvas as vast as American history.

How to choose the book's topics became the first issue of concern.

Certain subjects jumped out for coverage due to their fame or importance. Into this category fell items like September 11th, the Civil War and D-Day, and the character of George Washington.

Also obvious to address were vital documents and texts like the Constitution and Declaration of Independence and Abraham Lincoln's speeches.

A theme that emerged was the pioneering ethic, in the broadest sense, found threaded throughout the American story. This entails not only literal pioneering and exploration, as with Lewis and Clark and the California Gold Rush. As important, it dealt with pioneering innovation in technology and science, and in politics and social affairs. Thus the book features inventors and technologists such as Robert Fulton and Norman Borlaug, the latter the late-twentieth-century deviser of "miracle grains." Important events in innovation like the Manhattan Project and the creation of the digital computer are also covered. America is revealed as the nation of firsts.

In this vein, the book also covers "social pioneers" such as Frederick Douglass and Helen Keller, various business innovators, and artistic creators like Walt Disney. Biographies make up a large part of the book, and their subjects' ability to overcome seemingly impossible difficulties to attain their often-noble goals is a constant theme.

Since the "Great Recession" of recent years, economics has become a greater concern in U.S. politics, and history. So I found it enlightening to trace, from the founding of the country to today, the federal role, at least, in areas like banking, taxes, and infrastructure, the latter term referring things like canals, highways, rails, and electronic communications.

Although the book stresses "high politics"—famous leaders and battles—and "high technology"—noted technical breakthroughs, before and through today's computerized "high tech"—I tried to round things out. So a number of sections deal with the sweep of American culture: its religion, literature, sports, immigration over the ages, and even its cuisine.

This is a popular work of history, meant to entertain as well as inform. Pulling out a page from the poet Virgil, I've often started out a chapter in *media res,* in the middle of the action, of a crisis or a discovery, to draw the reader in and to bring the history alive.

The intended audience is the general reader, especially those interested in history, politics, and popular science and culture. Further, the book can serve as a background reader to students, middle school and up, who are first sinking their teeth into the American saga. Today the media is replete with reports of public ignorance about essential aspects of the national history. Perhaps this book can serve in a small way as antidote.

Despite the many problems and challenges America has faced, the book is optimistic in tone. At a time of seeming national decline, when the country's attention too often seems to be on the latest foibles of the shallowest of celebrities, it aims to inspire. There was plenty of inspirational material to mine.

The book focuses largely on heroic events and creative individuals who surmounted great difficulties to achieve great things—for instance, going to the moon, wiring the planet, defeating the Nazis, abolishing slavery, setting up the first large democratic republic, and largely banishing starvation overseas, to name some achievements—of which no other nation can boast. These exceptional tales are America's to tell.

Finally, some words of thanks. I am very grateful to Turner's editors for patiently putting up with my blowing through one hard-and-fast deadline after another, then for shepherding the work through its later stages. And to the Turner team, for their innovative notions on marketing and publicity. Finally to the publisher, Mr. Todd Bottorff, whose business-savvy approach at Turner is bringing new promise to the "old media" of books in our dynamic, digital age.

APOLLO:
THE MISSIONS TO THE MOON

I believe that this nation should commit itself to achieving the goal, before this decade is out, of landing a man on the Moon and returning him safely to the Earth." Thus stated President John F. Kennedy to a joint session of Congress on May 25, 1961, jumpstarting a gigantic effort to build and send manned spaceships to Earth's satellite.

COSMIC CATCH-UP

Kennedy was playing catch-up, in a Cold War space race with the United States' archrival, the Soviet Union. In November 1957, the Soviets had been the first to launch a satellite, *Sputnik,* into

Earth's orbit. And just six weeks after, the Soviets launched the first "cosmonaut" into orbit—the dog Laika, nicknamed "Muttnik" by the Western media.

The civilian agency the National Aeronautics and Space Administration, or NASA, moved to carry out the youthful president's vision, called "Apollo," after the Greek god of light. At Florida's Cape Canaveral, an Air Force missile base was transformed into a sprawling launch site. It hosted the 130 million-cubic-foot Vehicle Assembly Building, for a time the world's largest structure by volume, to construct the towering rockets for boosting astronauts into space. Canaveral would be renamed the Kennedy Space Center in 1963, after President Kennedy's assassination.

NASA conducted Apollo research at far-flung centers. These included two that tested landing in the Moon's airless, gravity-free setting: the Langley Research Center in Hampton, Virginia, and the Dryden Flight Research Center, in Antelope Valley, California. Vice President Lyndon B. Johnson, from Texas, placed Apollo's headquarters, the Manned Spacecraft Center, in Houston; the Center was later renamed the Johnson Space Center.

SKY-HIGH BUDGET, AND AMBITION

Over the course of its fifteen-year life, Apollo would cost about $24 billion, or in 2010 dollars, $190 billion—about ten times the size of NASA's current single-year budget. NASA's Washington-wise chief, James E. Webb—a former head of the Bureau of the Budget and ranking aide to a congressman and governor—cut deals with the relevant Capitol Hill committees to fund Apollo's substantial budget. The project contracted with some 20,000 firms and universities, and employed about 400,000 workers.

The program's éminence grise was Wernher von Braun, who had designed Germany's V-2 rocket, the first long-range missile, during the Second World War. At war's end, under top-secret "Operation Paperclip," U.S. military intelligence spirited von Braun and his best engineers to America. For the moon mission, the scientist was tapped to lead the George C. Marshall Space Flight Center, in Huntsville, Alabama. There, his men designed the *Saturn V*—the most powerful rocket ever built. The three-stage, 363-foot-high, liquid-fuel-burning beast reached speeds exceeding 15,000 mph, and threw out 7,500,000 pounds of thrust. When newscaster Walter Cronkite watched a *Saturn* test launch from six miles away, vibrations from the takeoff nearly shook apart his broadcast booth.

For a time, von Braun clashed with George Mueller from NASA's Office of Manned Space Flight, who was brought in from successful Air Force missile projects to slash Apollo's costs and red tape. Although von Braun wanted to methodically test the *Saturn* stage by stage, Mueller ordered him to test the rocket's three stages all at once, saving time and money. "It sounded reckless," von Braun concluded, "but [his] reasoning was impeccable."

THREE BIG STEPS

The moon program consisted of three successive manned projects, of gradually increasing ambition. The first was Project Mercury, lasting from 1961 into 1963. It launched small, one-man capsules into space for short periods, giving NASA valuable information on space flight and its effect on humans. In 1962, Mercury astronaut John Glenn, a U.S. Marine aviator, became the first American to orbit the Earth.

The second project was Gemini: in 1965–66 it launched pairs of astronauts for orbital fights lasting up to almost four days. Gemini had the first computers used on a spacecraft. Its astronauts gained experience with critical tasks like docking spacecraft in orbit. In March 1966, during the *Gemini 8* mission, an errant thruster whirled the spacecraft wildly in orbit, before commander Neil Armstrong regained control to make an emergency "splashdown" in the ocean.

The program culminated with Project Apollo's flights to the Moon. The Apollo spacecraft included a Command Module, for journeying close to the Moon after the *Saturn V* put the craft in high Earth orbit, and a Lunar Module, which separated from the Command Module to land on and take off from the Moon.

In January 1967, *Apollo 1*'s three astronauts—Virgil "Gus" Grissom, Roger Chaffee, Jr., and Edward White II—boarded the spacecraft for a test. Engineers heard an astronaut's voice cry out from the launch pad, "We've got a fire in the cockpit!" A blaze ignited by faulty wiring engulfed their cabin, suffocating the men.

NASA suspended the program for over 18 months. Technicians and contractors pored over every detail of the craft, redesigning much of it.

Three Memorable Missions

Apollo recovered, shifting from crisis to triumph. Three successful missions stood out.

In December 1968, the *Apollo 8* astronauts—James Lovell, Jr., Frank Borman, and William Anders—became the first men to journey to the Moon. From 60 miles above the surface, they orbited Earth's satellite 10 times, observing its never-before-viewed far side. They were also the first to photograph an "Earth rise"—an ocean-blue Earth emerging over the lunar horizon.

On Christmas Eve, while beaming their startling images back to Earth, Anders transfixed a worldwide audience with words from Genesis: "In the beginning God created the heaven and the Earth . . . and God saw that it was good . . . And from the crew of *Apollo 8* we close with . . . a Merry Christmas and God bless all of you—all of you on the good Earth."

On July 20, 1969, *Apollo 11* became the first manned craft to land on the Moon. From lunar orbit, astronauts Neil Armstrong and Edwin Buzz Aldrin, Jr., detached their Lunar Module from the Command Module, piloted by astronaut Michael Collins, and descended to the surface. Stepping on the Moon's dust and rocks, Armstrong famously stated: "That's one small step for man, one giant leap for mankind." Televised images of the landing and the astronauts' "Moon walk" were beamed back to a spellbound audience of 600 million.

On April 13, 1970, *Apollo 13* was 200,000 miles outbound from Earth. Suddenly, an onboard oxygen tank exploded, rendering its Command Module inhabitable, and imperiling the lives of the crew. Commander James Lovell tersely informed the Manned Spacecraft Center: "Houston, we've got a problem." Engineers, managers, and the astronauts scrambled to find a fix as the public, and the anxious astronauts' wives, watched and waited.

Improvising, the crew powered down the Command Module and took refuge in the Lunar Module. There, shivering, they conserved scarce supplies of heat and water. The biggest threat was the buildup of carbon dioxide, potentially leading to asphyxiation. The Lunar Module lacked sufficient canisters of lithium hydroxide to filter out the carbon dioxide. However, engineers conducted a scheme to connect to the Command Module's ample canisters of lithium hydroxide with an air hose.

The crew, meantime, took its craft, short of fuel, around the Moon, using its gravitational force as a "slingshot" to propel *Apollo 13* back to Earth. Despite fears the initial explosion had damaged its heat shield, the Command Module splashed down safely six days after launch.

As Kennedy had noted in his 1961 speech: "We choose to go to the Moon, not because [such things] are easy, but because they are hard."

MOONSET

In 1971–72, three more Moon landings took place; astronauts deployed a wheeled Lunar Rover for moving about on the rocky surface. But a weakening economy and a budget crunch cancelled the other three planned missions. Von Braun's dream of a follow-up mission to Mars was replaced by the less adventuresome, and problem-plagued, Space Shuttle.

Still, the "Space Age" that Apollo ushered in changed life on Earth far beyond the program's more mundane spinoffs like Velcro and freeze-dried food. Today, satellites at light speed give us our news, travel routes, and weather predictions. The smaller computers developed for going to the Moon spurred further miniaturization, and today's ubiquitous handheld devices. And other NASA programs, deep-space telescopes and probes, have revealed the age and content of the universe, and some of the mysteries of its creation.

ARLINGTON:
THE NATION'S CEMETERY

The place has a pedigree befitting the nation's most renowned burial ground. Located in Virginia across the Potomac from the city of Washington, its rolling 624 acres spread out from the Arlington House mansion, originally owned by George Washington Parke Custis. He was the adopted grandson of George Washington, the nation's first commander-in-chief, and the grandson of Martha Washington from her first marriage. Custis and his wife had one child, Mary Anna, who inherited their estate in 1857.

FROM MANSION GROUNDS TO RESTING PLACE

In 1831, at Arlington House, Mary Anna had married U.S. Army officer Robert E. Lee, the son of Revolutionary War hero

Henry "Light Horse Harry" Lee. The younger Lee, later the superintendent of the U.S. Military Academy at West Point, and future
ranking general of the Confederate Army, was the estate's executor
until 1861, with the advent of the Civil War. Lee and Mary Anna
left Arlington House, and Federal troops took over the property,
after Mrs. Lee could not be present to pay the property taxes. Her
husband expressed a hope that the slaves on the estate, according to
Custis' will, would be educated and freed.

Commanding the troops on the mansion's ground was Gen.
Montgomery Meigs, the Union Army's Quartermaster General.
Meigs was charged with housing, transporting, and feeding the
Union forces, and in that role efficiently dispensed the then-stagger-
ing sum of $1.5 billion in military contracts. In the 1830s, ironically,
Meigs and fellow Army lieutenant and engineer Robert E. Lee had
together surveyed the Mississippi River.

In 1863, President Lincoln dedicated the first national military
cemetery, at Gettysburg. As the war's military deaths swelled toward
a final toll of 625,000, the need for more burial sites grew. Meantime,
Meigs had grown bitter toward Lee and the Confederacy over the
war. In 1864, he wrote to Secretary of War Edwin Stanton, suggest-
ing that the environs of Arlington House be made into a cemetery.
"The grounds about the mansion are admirably adapted to such a
use," Meigs noted.

Stanton agreed, and an initial 200 acres near Arlington House
was so designated. In August 1864, twenty-six soldiers were transferred from a Union morgue and interred in the rose garden of the
Lee manse, as Meigs looked on. By war's end, 16,000 were buried at
Arlington, including 2,111 soldiers in the mass grave of the "Tomb
of the Unknown Dead from the Civil War." Gen. Meigs's son, killed
in action by rebel soldiers, was himself buried in the cemetery, as was
Meigs on his death in 1892.

Gravesite of the Famous and the Famously Unknown

By 2010, over 300,000 were buried there, including the cremated remains of over 38,000 persons. The honored dead include representatives of every U.S. conflict from the American Revolution to Afghanistan. Over 6,000 are interred every year. Active duty service personnel, or retired or veteran personnel, and their spouses, widows, and children, are eligible for burial. Since 1968, Arlington National Cemetery has become a natural place for American presidents, almost every year, to deliver a Memorial Day address on the nation's veterans from the Memorial Amphitheater.

The military cemetery contains many of the country's most famous soldiers. These include Army Chief of Staff and later Secretary of State George Marshall, and the First World War's General of the Armies, John "Black Jack" Pershing. The cemetery also holds, on a rise overlooking the Capitol, the resting spot of Pierre Charles L'Enfant, who drew up the architectural plans for Washington, D.C. Two Army sergeants, heavyweight champion Joe Louis, and Dashiell Hammett, author of *The Maltese Falcon,* are among the dead known more for their non-military exploits.

A number of memorials mark famous or infamous events. A tribute to the 184 persons killed in the September 11, 2001 attack on the Pentagon is in the shape of that five-sided building. A striking memorial was built from the mast of the USS *Maine,* and its 266 dead crewmen, whose sinking in Havana Harbor in 1898 touched off the Spanish-American War. There are also memorials for the crews of the *Challenger* and *Columbia* Space Shuttle disasters.

The most visited place is the burial site of President John Kennedy, laid to rest there after his assassination in 1963. An "eternal flame" honors the spot. Nearby is the grave of his widow, First Lady Jacqueline Bouvier Kennedy Onassis, and his brother, Senator Robert Kennedy, also assassinated in office.

Famously un-famous are the several soldiers buried at the Tomb of the Unknowns, a 79-ton marble vault honoring unidentified combatants. Since 1948, elite, immaculately dressed members of the 3rd U.S. Infantry Regiment, "the Old Guard," have watched over the tomb day and night. Each hour or half hour, on public view, the sentries are relieved and replaced, to keep the honored dead ever under watch.

CLARA BARTON,
ANGEL OF THE BATTLEFIELD

It was the bloodiest day in American history. The lines of Union and Confederate soldiers stood but 50 yards apart, and bullets flew so thick they cut down the surrounding cornfields like a power mower. Army surgeons, running out of supplies, staunched wounds with cornhusks.

WARRIOR NURSE

Into the exploding shells and swirling clouds of gunpowder rolled some supply wagons and their mules and drivers. They were headed up by a dark-haired woman in a dark dress, bonnet, and red bow. She directed her teamsters to carry piles of bandages to the physicians.

On the makeshift hospital of someone's porch, stricken men were dabbed with ether for surgery. The woman bent down to offer one soldier a drink, then noticed a hole in her sleeve.

"A rifle ball had passed between my body and the right arm which supported him," recalled the Angel of the Battlefield, as the lady was henceforth known. "It cut through the sleeve and passed through his chest. There was no more to be done for him . . . I have never mended that hole in my sleeve."

She had pushed her mule teams all night to reach the fray, then cared for the men throughout the day, then supplied lanterns to the doctors at night. Finally, as the Civil War battle of Antietam wound down, Clara Barton—later to found the American Red Cross—collapsed from exhaustion and typhoid fever.

IMPROBABLE UPBRINGING

The person who became America's most influential caregiver had an unlikely childhood. Born in 1821 in Oxford, Massachusetts, Barton was short, spoke with a lisp, and was intensely shy. She was a fast learner, however: her brothers and sisters taught her math and reading, and how to ride bareback. Yet she was so afflicted by nervousness that she could barely eat. About the house she took in tales of her great-aunt, Martha, a midwife who'd delivered about one thousand babies in the town of Hallowell (now Augusta), Maine.

When Clara was 11, her brother David suffered a terrible accident, falling from the rafters of the family barn. He took over two years to recover, and during this time Clara learned how to administer all his medicines and therapies, including the "great, loathsome, crawling leeches," then used to draw "bad blood" from patients.

Her parents urged the bright young lady, in her late teens, to overcome her shyness by teaching. Barton started out by instructing forty young men and women at a district school, with some of the males her age—and many rambunctious too. But "when they found I was as agile as themselves," she recalled, and "that my throw was as sure and as straight, their respect knew no bounds." Later, residing in a New Jersey town, she noticed knots of idle youngsters milling about, and offered to teach them without pay. Her effort turned into New Jersey's first free public school. Enrollment climbed from six students to over two hundred within a year.

A PATRIOT'S BLOODLINE

Barton's father had regaled her with tales of his service in the Revolutionary War, with heroic general "Mad" Anthony Wayne. So when the Civil War broke out, she reflected: "What could I do but go with the soldiers, or work for them and my country? The patriot blood of my father was warm in my veins."

She started small and built up. In 1861, Barton was working as a patent recorder in Washington, D.C., when the battle of Fort Sumter in South Carolina touched off the war. In Baltimore, Southern sympathizers had attacked and wounded Union troops heading from up north to the capital city. Barton cared for the seriously injured at her sister's house, and brought the men food and clothes collected from Washington merchants.

When casualties swelled after the First Battle of Manassas, she asked ladies aid committees to gather and package supplies for convalescing soldiers. For Antietam, and the battle of Fredericksburg, she wangled a quartermaster's pass from the Army, and permission to take her mule teams through the battle lines, caring for Union and Confederate soldiers alike. "I may be compelled to face danger, but never fear it," she stated, "and while our soldiers can stand and fight, I can stand and feed and nurse them." In between bouts of depression, Barton was appointed to increasingly higher responsibilities in field hospitals.

By war's end, the nation needed to locate and identify tens of thousands of missing soldiers, many in unmarked mass graves. For this aim, President Lincoln sent out a missive: "To the Friends of Missing Persons: Miss Clara Barton has kindly offered to search for the missing prisoners of war. Please address her . . . giving her the name, regiment, and company of any missing prisoner."

Over four years, Barton answered 63,000 letters, and placed queries and lists of the missing in newspapers. She was much aided by a Union soldier, Dorence Atwater, who'd been in Georgia's infamous Andersonville Prison. Atwater managed to hand-copy and sneak out a list of approximately 13,000 men who'd died there. Barton ended up identifying more than 22,000 missing combatants.

POSTWAR EXPANSION

After the war, Barton often spoke on behalf of women's suffrage, appearing onstage with famous leaders like Susan B. Anthony. In front of veterans' organizations, she'd plead: "Soldiers! I have worked for you . . . God only knows women were your friends in time of peril and you should be theirs now." But the war had broken her health, and her doctors persuaded her to go recuperate in Europe.

While there, hostilities broke out between France and German-speaking Prussia. Far from resting, Barton established assistance centers in war-ravaged towns. She learned about Europe's incipient Red Cross movement, which set up national societies to aid wartime victims under a flag of neutrality.

On returning home in 1873, she was extremely ill for three years. Yet by 1877 she was lobbying the government to set up a U.S. branch of the Red Cross. In 1881, as Barton turned 60, the American Red Cross was established, with her as president.

Barton successfully pushed the Red Cross to expand its work into natural disasters. Indeed, during her 23-year tenure, her organization helped the victims of some of the worst disasters in American history. In 1889, she and 50 aid workers were among the first to aid survivors of the devastating Johnstown, Pennsylvania flood. In 1900, Barton founded an orphanage for the children of the 6,000 people killed by the Galveston, Texas hurricane.

As Barton turned 83, criticism mounted over her age and slap-dash administration of Red Cross records. In 1904, she resigned her post.

However, she again bounced back. Barton set up the National First Aid Association of America, a step toward the now-common availability of first-aid kits and defibrillators in public places.

In 1912, at age 90, the Angel of the Battlefield died in Glen Echo, Maryland, surrounded by many friends.

An Outsized Legacy

The famous organization she founded was to explode in size and responsibilities. During the First World War, the adult membership of the Red Cross grew from 17,000 to 20 million. In the Second World War, it collected 13 million pints of blood for the U.S. Armed Services. By the twenty-first century, the Red Cross supplied 50 percent of America's blood, was the principal private provider of mass care in national emergencies, and worked closely with foreign-country branches to address overseas disasters from Haitian earthquakes to Japanese tsunamis.

Alexander Graham Bell:
"Innovator: Get Me Long Distance"

Presidents had no Secret Service, and often no bodyguards, back in 1881. So when an assassin with a loaded pistol stepped up to President Garfield at a downtown Washington train depot that July, the Chief Executive had no defense. Shot twice at point-blank range, Garfield was soon fighting for his life.

Yankee ingenuity emerged, as some of the country's best thinkers fought to save the President's life. A team of Navy engineers put together a prototype air-conditioner to blow cool air over the sweating, bedridden Garfield. In trying to locate and remove a bullet buried in Garfield's abdomen, doctors turned to a 34-year-old scientist, who quickly devised the first metal detector.

Due to the metal in the President's bed frame, the detector failed in its task. But Americans saddened by the Garfield tragedy thought back with pride to the scientist's great triumph in Boston five years before.

A Master of Speech Trains with the Deaf

The man, named Aleck, born and raised in Scotland, had accompanied his family to Canada in 1870 after a tragedy of his own. Both his brothers had died of tuberculosis, and he himself had contracted the disease. His father took his son Aleck, along with the rest of the family, to recuperate in Ontario.

Adept in many fields, Aleck was a noted instructor of sign language to deaf-mute students. After regaining his health, he traveled to Boston, and in 1872 set up the School of Vocal Physiology and Mechanics of Speech.

Communication skills ran deep in his family. His grandfather was an actor. His father was the author of a well-known book on teaching the deaf to lip-read and to speak. His mother, though herself deaf, was a skilled pianist.

As a youth, Aleck and a friend constructed, from scraps of rubber and wood, a toy robot that could enunciate words like "mama." Playing with the family terrier, Aleck got it to make English-like sounds by manipulating its vocal chords and lips. In Boston, one of his handicapped students was the blind-and-deaf child turned author, Helen Keller. He spent much of his free time tinkering with telegraphs and other electrical devices.

Long-distance communications were then in the hands of the telegraph companies, who were eager to cut costs by finding a way of sending multiple messages at once. In 1873, Aleck decided to focus on his research in that field. He cut back his students to two:

six-year-old Georgie Sanders and 15-year-old Mabel Hubbard—the fathers of both girls bankrolled his extracurricular work.

Laboring for long hours in his workshop, nagged by headaches, Aleck came upon a new way of communication by wire—with the human voice.

Voices from out of Nowhere

Aleck fashioned a device where material stretched across a mouthpiece vibrates from the speaker's voice, causing fluctuations in a magnet's current, which a faraway receiver translates back into sound. Helping him make test models was 22-year-old electrician Thomas Watson.

On March 12, 1876, while toiling in his lab, Aleck called out to Watson, who was working down the hall next to the receiver of their experimental "telephone." Watson clearly heard Aleck's words coming out of the receiver: "Mr. Watson, come here, I want to see you!" For the first time, the human voice had been sent over a wire.

Five days before, Alexander "Aleck" Graham Bell had applied for a patent for his invention in Washington, D.C. That same day, an accomplished, rival inventor, engineer Elisha Gray, filed for a similar device at the same patent office. Bell was granted rights for "the method of, and apparatus for, transmitting vocal or other sounds telegraphically by causing electrical undulations, similar in form to the vibrations of the air." Historians dispute whether Bell or Gray first invented the telephone, although Bell spent more time developing and demonstrating it. The brilliant Gray went on to invent the first fax machine, for a company later acquired by Xerox Corp.

In June 1876, Bell made the first public demonstration of the telephone, at Philadelphia's Centennial Exposition marking America's hundredth year of independence. Among those watching was Brazilian Emperor Dom Pedro II, who cried out, "My God, it talks!"

As Popular as the iPhone

In 1877, the Bell Telephone Company was founded. Bell and his backers—Mr. Hubbard and Mr. Sanders—offered their telephone patent to telegraph giant Western Union for $100,000. However, the company's chief thought the device a mere curiosity. Several years later, as phone use grew, he decided the patent was actually worth over $25 million, but Bell and his fellow stakeholders, now millionaires, were no longer selling. By 1887, 150,000 Americans owned telephones. In ensuing years, 600 lawsuits were brought against Bell Telephone, alleging patent infringement; the company won them all.

Famous and financially set, Bell married his old student, Mabel Hubbard, giving her 1,487 of his 1,497 shares of Bell Telephone stock. Wrung out from work and constant courtroom patent testimony, he resigned from his namesake company. In 1882, he became a naturalized U.S. citizen, later stating, "I am not one of those hyphenated Americans who claim allegiance to two countries."

The Necessity of Invention

He accomplished much more before his death in 1922. In 1915, a hydrofoil he designed set the world marine speed record at 70.9 mph. Decades prior, he dreamed up the "photophone," which transmitted voice by vibrating beams of light. Though little used at the time, it was the first wireless phone, and anticipated optical-fiber transmission and the Droid by a century.

"Leave the beaten track behind occasionally," Bell once noted, "and dive into the woods. Every time you do you will be certain to find something that you have never seen before."

NORMAN BORLAUG:
HE SAVED MORE LIVES THAN ANY OTHER AMERICAN

He was a champion wrestler, and a brilliant botanist, and he needed all his strength and smarts that hot summer of 1965. Norman Borlaug had 35 truckloads of miracle grain to get to the world's starving masses, but he kept running into one obstacle after another. First the supply of high-yield wheat, which he'd cultivated in Mexico, was stopped by the Mexican police. Then U.S. border guards tried enforcing a ban on imported grains. Eventually the trucks of the noted agronomist approached the port of Los Angeles. But due to the Watts race riots then devastating the city, National Guards troops halted the caravan. Finally, the vehicles got to the harbor, and the grain was shipped to famine-plagued India and Pakistan.

Yet after the wheat arrived in the Indian subcontinent, more bad news emerged. "I went to bed thinking the problem was at last solved," recalled Borlaug, "and woke up to the news that war had broken out between India and Pakistan." With artillery at times flashing nearby, Borlaug and his aides distributed the precious seed to native farmers.

THE GREEN REVOLUTION

His efforts paid off. That year, despite delays in planting, wheat yields in Pakistan rose 70 percent. And the next year, 98 percent. In less than a decade India's vast population, for generations stricken by mass starvation, could feed itself.

Many said it couldn't be done. Population was rising swiftly around the world from health measures like mass vaccinations, and some feared food supplies couldn't keep up. Biologist Paul Ehrlich, author of the 1968 best-selling book *The Population Bomb*, stated: "In the 1970s and 1980s hundreds of millions of people will starve to death in spite of any crash programs embarked upon now."

Yet China, another country wracked by millions of deaths from famine, also planted Borlaug's "miracle grain," and went on to stamp out malnutrition. In ensuing years, thousands of Borlaug-trained scientists produced high-yield rice and other grains and brought them to the Middle East and South America, also drastically changing these areas' food output and nutrition for the good.

Because of Borlaug's "Green Revolution," farmers worldwide could feed six times as many people in 2000 as they could have fed on roughly the same amount of cultivated land in 1900. The strains of new high-yield grain saved as many as one billion lives.

Further, they spared an immense amount of virgin land from development. "Without high-yield agriculture," Borlaug later noted, "increases in food output would have been realized through drastic expansion of acres under cultivation—[with] losses of pristine land a hundred times greater than all losses to urban and suburban expansion."

Small-Town Rassler, Big-Time Thinker

Born in 1914, the son of immigrants fleeing a famine-ravaged Norway, Borlaug was raised on a small farm in Iowa. Shocked by the region's Dust Bowl–era storms, he became convinced that scientific farming could avoid similar calamities. He put himself through the University of Minnesota (UM) by working in the fields for 50 cents a day. A vigorous and muscular man, he joined the wrestling team, and was eventually inducted into the NCAA Wrestling Hall of Fame. After a stint in the U.S. Forest Service, he attended a lecture on plant diseases by Dr. Elvin Stakman, who envisioned going "further than has ever been possible to eradicate the miseries of hunger." Borlaug immediately signed up for UM's Ph.D. program in plant pathology.

In the 1940s, the young scientist, after receiving funding from the Dupont Corp. and the Ford and Rockefeller foundations, became director of Mexico's International Maize and Wheat Improvement Center. For over 13 years, he and his fellow researchers strove to develop a disease-resistant strain of wheat. To speed things up, they employed "shuttle breeding," where after one season of cultivation up north they'd race to southern Mexico for a second period of hybridization. When their heavy-grained wheat caused its long stalks to droop, they interbred it with a Japanese dwarf variety. The result: a stocky, pest-resistant, nutrition-rich grain that could thrive almost anywhere.

In 1970, Borlaug was awarded the Nobel Peace Prize. Busily working in a remote Mexican field when his wife told him of the honor, he refused to take time off to drive to a phone, making reporters travel several hours to interview him personally.

Over the next four decades, before his death in 2009 at age 95, and as a professor in soil and crop science at Texas A&M, Borlaug spread the gospel of the Green Revolution to Africa and other realms. In his long life he arguably saved more lives than anyone else in history.

THE CAJUNS:
SOUTH TO AMERICA

Church was the last place where they expected to be run out of their own country. On a Sunday in August 1755, while many were attending services, the expulsion order was read aloud to 12,000 French-speaking Canadians. To future Americans, they would be known for their spicy seafood cuisine and foot-stomping Zydeco concerts. But for the moment, they were still inhabitants of l'Acadie, the French, and soon-to-be British, provinces of Nova Scotia, New Brunswick, and Prince Edward Island.

EXODUS, PART I

The denizens of those coastal lands were ordered down to the docks, where ships from colonial Boston waited to scatter them throughout Britain's far-flung colonies. Like in a slave sale, families were separated on the spot and sent packing to distant, disparate shores, from New England to the Falkland Islands. To goad a speedy departure, British troops burned down their villages. Land was seized and handed to Crown loyalists from the Scottish Highlands.

The refugees were displaced as part of the "Seven Years War," called the French and Indian War by Americans, which started the year of the expulsion. After an assault that year on New Brunswick's Fort Beauséjour, the British had found among the French defenders many of these Acadians, a people who refused to swear allegiance to the British crown. The British troops in Acadie, considerably outnumbered, dreaded a local rising. So they engaged in an "ethnic cleansing" of the natives.

The royal governor, Charles Lawrence, wrote a garrison commander: "Use all the means proper and necessary for collecting the people together so as to get them on board . . . depriving those who shall escape of all means of shelter or support by burning their houses and destroying everything that may afford them the means of subsistence."

During the eight years of the resulting Le Grand Dérangement, the Great Upheaval, 10,000 were exiled. Many perished from disease aboard crowded boats. On finally reaching their destinations, they were often shunned. Some 3,500 returned to their ancestral homes in France, where the natives jeered them as foreigners. Over 860 went to Britain, where many ended in prison. Over 660 went to Connecticut, over a thousand to Massachusetts. But most of the American colonies threw the Frenchmen out.

Exodus, Part II

Some headed to French settlements, about 2,000 to the province of Quebec. Another spot offering a kinder reception was Louisiana, then run by Spain, a foe of Britain. Its leaders recognized 2,500 or more of the newcomers as fellow Catholics, and anti-English bulwarks. Indeed, during the American Revolution two decades later, 600 formerly French-Canadian militiamen were to help wrest Baton Rouge from Britain.

The Spanish governors of Louisiana directed the French Canadians to settle at strategic spots along the Mississippi, and later the marshlands west of New Orleans, and prairies further west. They gave the destitute arrivals some land, supplies, and guns, and lent them engineers to survey suitable places for settling down.

Word trickled out to fellow exiles of Louisiana's hospitality. Many set sail for New Orleans. In that then-huge territory, some were to settle as far north as the Dakotas. The arrivistes—hardy trappers, fishermen, farmers—adapted to the new setting. In the swamp of the Atchafalaya Basin they hunted alligator and collected oysters and crawfish, grew rice, and fought off malaria and yellow fever. On drier land they raised cane and cattle.

In Louisiana, they were called Cajuns, an anglicized form of Acadie, possibly from the Canadian-Indian place name cadique, "a good place to camp." Along the sprawling bayous and ranchlands the Cajuns interbred with the native-born Spanish or French, known as Creoles, and with the Germans settling north of New Orleans, bringing with them accordions which the Cajuns adopted for their distinctive music. About them were colorfully garbed Native Americans from the marshlands, slaves, and formerly slave "free men of color," American whites pouring in after the purchase of Louisiana, even Filipinos disembarking from Spanish galleons out of Manila.

Much later, the Cajuns had to struggle a second time to save themselves and their culture. In the 1910s, state and local governments banned their distinctive French dialect from the public schools. At the same time the life-loving, largely blue-collar Cajuns were looked down on as "unwashed" country folk by the sophisticated Creoles of Crescent City.

CAJUN IS COOL

Beginning in the 1950s, as part of the growing American move-ment in ethnic roots, Cajun culture made a comeback. By 2000, Ca-jun was cool. Zydeco music and "blackened" seafood became American staples, and even bayou literature was big, with the novels of detective Dave Robicheaux perennial best-sellers.

Today, some 600,000 Americans are eager to claim the ancestry of "Acadian driftwood"—the formerly dispossessed of Canada's maritime provinces.

THE CHOSIN RESERVOIR:
WINTER HEROICS IN WAR-TORN KOREA

The GIs figured they'd be back home well in time for Thanksgiving, not to mention Christmas. In October 1950, the Korean War was all but over, it seemed, after just four months.

That June, North Korean forces had invaded South Korea. But after a surprise, behind-their-backs landing at Inchon, Korea, Allied forces under U.S. Gen. Douglas MacArthur had pushed the North Koreans up to the Yalu River, on Korea's border with China.

THE SHIFTING FORTUNES OF WAR

Yet, as the coldest Korean winter in decades approached, vast armies from Communist China, allies of North Korea, rushed across the Yalu. Advancing quickly, by late November they had cut off the American and Allied forces strung out along the 12-mile-long Chosin Reservoir.

On the west side of the frozen body of water were the U.S. Marines. On the east side were the U.S. Army, some Royal Marines from the UK, and South Korean units, making up "Task Force Faith."

Greatly outnumbered, the Allied forces began a ferocious, fighting "retreat" to south of the reservoir, and to the safety of the coast and waiting ships.

Actually, as the Marine commander, General Oliver Prince (O.P.) Smith, stated at the time: "Retreat? Hell, we're attacking in a different direction!"

Temperatures fell to 35 degrees below zero. Signal flares wouldn't go off, the metal of mortars cracked. The blood from wounds froze in place. Many more were injured from frostbite than bullets.

The poet John Kent described it this way:

How deep the cold takes us down,
into the searing frost of hell;
where mountain snows,
unyielding winds, strip our flesh,
(and) bare our bones.

HUMAN WAVE ATTACKS

Chosin was the battle where the world learned about "human wave attacks." At the sound of a bugle, hordes of enemy infantry would charge. Many attackers were sent into battle without weapons, and would scrounge for a rifle among their dead. In countless ambushes of the Allied convoys battling their way south, the enemy bayoneted the wounded lying in trucks, or set them afire with phosphorus grenades. The Marines, refusing to leave behind their dead, lashed the bodies of the fallen to trucks. Recalled Army Lieutenant Jerry McCabe: "Notwithstanding terror, we did our job . . . The Chinese thought they would destroy us. That didn't happen. They had taken horrible casualties. We stopped them and bloodied them."

On mountainous terrain, along primitive roads, men often fought on in isolated pockets, without leaders. The commander of the U.S. Army troops, Colonel Alan McLean, was killed; he was the highest ranking U.S. fatality in the war. His successor, Lt. Colonel Don Faith, was also killed.

A Contagion of Courage

Courage was common. Seventeen men earned the Medal of Honor, including Lt. Col. Faith.

Another Medal winner was Marine Reserve Private Hector Cafferata. When an enemy regiment attacked his company, every man in his fire unit was wounded and knocked out of action. Exposing himself to withering fire, Cafferata single-handedly stopped the assault. In another attack that same morning, he seized a grenade that had fallen among his comrades, and hurled it away as it exploded, badly wounding his hand and arm. Ignoring intense pain, he continued to fight, until a sniper's bullet finally forced him to the sidelines.

The valor of so many individuals resulted in honors for their units. The 1st Marine Division received a Presidential Unit Citation in 1952; Task Force Faith got one in 2000.

About 3,000 American and Allied soldiers lost their lives at Chosin. Many thousands more were wounded or suffered from the blackened skin or amputations of frostbite.

Yet they achieved their mission. Due to the sacrifice of some, the bulk of the forces broke through the enemy, and made it to the port of Hungnam. From there, by late December, they were evacuated to safety, along with the perhaps 98,000 Korean civilians they rescued. Many of the veterans of Chosin lived to fight another day, to save a future, democratic South Korea, until the armistice of 1953 brought fighting to a halt.

INVENTING THE COMPUTER:
MAUCHLY AND ECKERT

B uilding the world's first digital computer—at the University of Pennsylvania's Moore School of Engineering from 1943 to 1945—wasn't easy.

Today's software suffers from "bugs"; hardware, back in the day, suffered from rodents. At the University, mice kept gnawing away at the circuitry of the thousand-square-foot machine. So, the project's leader, Dr. John Mauchly, put the mice in cages, put them on diets, then unleashed them on assorted brands of wires. Only wires that survived the nibbling were bought.

Another problem was the 17,000-plus vacuum tubes in the device, the Electronic Numerical Integrator and Computer, or ENIAC.

ENIAC would make a calculation error if any of the tubes failed, and the tubes were error-prone.

BORN TO COMPUTE

Mauchly's upbringing had prepared him for such challenging work. Born in 1907, he was raised in Chevy Chase, Maryland, while his physicist father did research on electrical fields at nearby Washington, D.C.'s Carnegie Institute. As a child, to read uninterrupted past his bedtime, Mauchly planted sensors outside his bedroom to warn of his parents' approach. To get phone service for his pals, he tapped into the neighborhood's telephone poles.

After a doctoral program in physics and engineering from Baltimore's Johns Hopkins University, Mauchly got a job doing research about sunspots. Frustrated at sifting through vast amounts of solar data by hand, he tinkered with ways of automating the information. Buying up packs of GE neon bulbs, he wired together digitized switches. After obtaining a professorship at the Moore School, he spent further long hours poring through technical magazines and soldering together circuits. Using a now-familiar binary system of ones and zeros, he added up numbers with pulses of electricity, then stored the numbers electronically without having to laboriously re-enter the data.

DYNAMIC DIGITAL DUO

In 1941, Mauchly began working with a 22-year-old Moore School engineering student, John Presper Eckert, Jr. The laid-back Mauchly excelled at theory; the eager Eckert, at putting theory into practice, and schematics to machine. The duo proved perfect complements.

By 1943, the United States had entered the Second World War. A pressing military need was faster ways of making "calculator tables," which contained the many factors, like wind speed and shell velocity, for firing artillery with accuracy. "The people using the guns," noted Eckert, "were having to make guesswork corrections on the tables to hit anything."

Mauchly claimed he could build a "computer" that would figure out a shell's trajectory in 100 seconds, by performing 1,000 calculations a second. The Army's Ballistic Research Laboratory, at Maryland's Aberdeen Proving Ground, told him to try.

Mauchly, Eckert, and 12 engineers built their complex machine at the Moore School over two-and-half-years, at a cost of $486,804. The 10-foot-tall ENIAC had 70,000 resistors, 10,000 capacitors, and 6,000 switches. Eckert got the 17,486 vacuum tubes to work, mostly without error, by fiddling with and reducing their voltage.

Souls of the New Machine

Card readers and card punches were employed for data entry and output. Manipulating the switches and cards were the first programmers—all of them women. Noted one: "Most of the men were away fighting, so we were left in charge."

The wartime team worked seven days a week, nicknaming their demanding construction the "MANIAC," but took out time for pranks. One night, after Eckert fell asleep next to the computer, two assistants carried him into an identical but empty room. When he awoke, he was certain ENIAC had been stolen.

The completed machine worked better than Mauchly had predicted, making 5,000 calculations in under a second, and figuring out the trajectory of a shell's arc in 20 seconds. When journalists assembled for a demonstration, they asked an engineer running ENIAC when the test calculation would take place—then realized it already had.

Mauchly and Eckert went on to found the first computer firm, invent the first usable programming language, and design the first commercial computer, the UNIVAC.

The giant, cumbersome machine they patched together in the 1940s was the progenitor of all the tiny, elegant processors of today.

THE CONSTITUTION:
A FEDERAL BLUEPRINT

Some major figures of the American Revolution, like George Mason, opposed it. From his diplomatic perch in France, Thomas Jefferson had grave doubts about the thing. So did Benjamin Franklin, in his seat at the 1787 Philadelphia convention drafting this constitution, or set of rules, for governing the 13 separate and newly independent states.

FOUNDING DOUBTERS

Many in the big and powerful states, like Virginia, felt they didn't need it. Many in the small states, like Rhode Island, felt they'd be trampled by the big states if they joined. In Pennsylvania, a mob had to drag two prominent opponents over to the state constitutional convention, so it could reach a quorum for voting in favor. At the convention, Franklin gazed at the image of a sun carved into the presiding officer's chair. With irony, he confessed that he couldn't tell "whether the sun was rising or setting."

Finally, after New York state's razor-thin vote for approval, the national convention ratified the document. Its adherents would have been astounded at how influential it eventually became, both in the U.S. and as a model for new governments abroad.

Framework for Governance

The U.S. Constitution lays out the structure and powers of the federal government and its relationship to the states.

Its Preamble, written by Governor Morris of Pennsylvania, states the Constitution's purpose: "We the People of the United States, in Order to form a more perfect Union, establish Justice, insure domestic Tranquility, provide for the common defence, promote the general Welfare, and secure the Blessings of Liberty to ourselves and our Posterity, do ordain and establish this Constitution for the United States of America."

Tripod System

The Constitution sets up three branches of government: the legislative, the executive, and the judicial.

The legislative branch, called Congress, is composed of two houses: the Senate, and the House of Representatives.

The Senate is comprised of Senators, two from each state, each elected for a term of six years.

The House is comprised of Representatives, or congressmen, their number by state based on the state's population, each elected for a term of two years. The House has the power to initiate all revenue and spending bills.

Among the other powers of Congress are: the ability to declare war, regulation of foreign commerce, establishment of rules on immigration and naturalization, and promotion of copyrights and patents.

The executive branch is composed of the President, or chief executive officer, elected to a four-year term, and supervising the departments and agencies making up that branch.

The President is the commander in chief of the armed forces. He has the power to propose legislation to Congress, and to veto laws passed by Congress, unless overridden by a two-thirds vote of both houses. The President can appoint ministers and "all other Officers of the United States." He also has the power to make treaties, with the "advice and consent" of the Senate.

The judicial branch consists of the Supreme Court and other federal courts. These courts mediate disputes between the states. The President nominates the members of the Supreme Court, and the Senate approves or rejects his nominations. The Supreme Court judges the constitutionality of Congress's laws and of the President's administrative actions.

Making Amendments

The Constitution may be altered by amendments to it, when approved by a two-thirds vote of both houses of Congress, and ratified by three quarters of the states.

As of 2011, there have been 27 amendments to the constitution. The initial 10 are the Bill of Rights. They include the right of free speech and of religion, the right to bear arms, the right to a trial by jury, the reservation to the states of powers not specified in the Constitution, and the prohibition against cruel and unusual punishment.

Other major amendments include:

13th—Abolishes slavery;

15th—Guarantees right to vote for all citizens;

16th—Gives Congress the power to levy an income tax;

18th—Prohibits the manufacture, sale, or transportation of "intoxicating liquors." (Was repealed by the 21st Amendment);

19th—Provides the right of women to vote;

24th—Forbids denial of voting rights due to failure to pay the so-called poll tax on an individual.

At 224 years and counting, the Constitution is the world's longest-running framework for a democratic republic.

D-Day:
Invasion of Europe

Sergeant John Steele of the 82nd Airborne Division watched with horror as the men of his regiment parachuted into the square of the German-occupied Norman French town of Sainte-Mère-Église, early that spring morning in 1944. During his own drop, Steele's parachute had gotten caught on the steeple of the town's church. From high above, he looked out helplessly as his fellow soldiers, defenseless, sailed down into the square. The defenders on the ground slaughtered them with rifles and machine guns.

Ten miles away, the 2nd Army Ranger Battalion tried the seemingly impossible: scaling the heavily guarded, 95-foot coastal cliffs of Pointe du Hoc, a German bastion whose massive 155-mm guns could dominate the coast below. On hitting the beach at the base of the cliff, they lost 15 men from single enemy machine gun. Then, as two destroyers offshore pinned down the defenders above, scores of rangers fired off grappling hooks and scrambled toward the top, their hands burnt from grasping extension ladders and slippery-wet ropes.

A VAST ARMADA

The paratroopers and rangers were a small part of D-Day (June 6, 1944), the first day of the Allied invasion of Nazi-occupied Europe during the Second World War. Taking place in Normandy, France, and consisting largely of American, British, and Canadian soldiers, airmen, and sailors, it was the largest invasion in world history.

The landings, which took place on five separate beaches stretching along 50 miles of Atlantic shore, included 144,829 troops. Landing further inland were 23,500 paratroopers, including the U.S. 82nd and 101st Airborne Divisions. The German defenders consisted of six infantry divisions and one panzer division.

Transporting and supporting the landings was the largest naval armada ever assembled. The U.S., British, and other navies manned 1,213 warships and deployed 3,500 landing craft.

Covering the skies over the invasion were over 13,000 Allied aircraft. Bombers and fighters launched over 11,000 sorties against hostile targets in and behind the invasion beaches.

Against the vast Allied air and sea forces, the small German air force and navy, worn down by months of targeted U.S. and British bombing, put up little fight.

GOOD FORTUNE, ADROIT DECEPTION

Heading the Allied forces was U.S. General Dwight Eisenhower. Due to poor weather, Eisenhower had agonized for days over whether or not to postpone the landings. His decision to move forward proved fortunate—the Germans had concluded that overcast skies made an invasion that day improbable. In fact, on invasion day, the German commander, the skilled field marshal Erwin Rommel, was in Germany for his wife's birthday, while German dictator Adolf Hitler slept through the morning.

The Supreme Allied Commander was also aided by a strategy of deception. In southeast England, opposite the French Pas de Calais coast where the Germans deemed an invasion most likely, the Allies constructed a "phantom army" of papier-mâché tanks and fake barracks, backed up by phony radio traffic and by many visits there by its "leader," U.S. Gen. George Patton, the Allied commander the Germans most feared. The ruse convinced the Germans that the invasion at Normandy was a feint.

Into the Teeth of the Foe

The landings went well in four of the five beaches but—as the book and movie *The Longest Day* and the film *Saving Private Ryan* depict—at Omaha Beach the Americans met fierce opposition from the experienced German 352nd Infantry Division. At Omaha Beach, the 1st Infantry Division grimly held together after taking massive casualties from direct enemy fire. "Two kinds of people are staying on this beach," Col. George Taylor told the soldiers, "the dead and those who are going to die. Now let's get the hell out of here." Specialists from the 6th Engineer Brigade blew up fortifications impeding the attackers, allowing infantry to seize the shoreline approaches.

At Pointe du Hoc, the rangers stormed the cliffs, destroyed the heavy guns nearby, and defended their position against repeated counterassault. At the Point and also at nearby Omaha Beach, where some had landed by mistake, they lost 135 killed and wounded out of 235. As for Sgt. Steele, the paratrooper at Ste. Mère-Eglise, he was rescued when other units of his division seized the town later that morning.

By midnight, all five beaches were secure. U.S. casualties were 1,465 dead, 1,928 missing and presumed dead, and 3,184 wounded.

Thereafter, massive Allied reinforcements poured into the beachheads, making likely Nazi Germany's final surrender, which occurred on May 8, 1945.

The Declaration of
Independence:
A Separate Nation

In early July 1776, America was on the verge of independence from Great Britain, and revolutionary leader John Adams of Massachusetts looked forward to making it official. Writing his wife Abigail, Adams made an accurate prophesy about future commemorations of Independence: "It will be celebrated, by succeeding Generations . . . with Pomp and Parade, with Shews, Games, Sports, Guns, Bells, Bonfires and Illuminations."

A FAIT ACCOMPLI

The 13 American colonies had engaged in a bloody war with Britain for over a year. In 1775 and early 1776, Americans had fought major battles with British Redcoats at Lexington, Concord, Bunker Hill in Massachusetts, Fort Ticonderoga in New York, and Quebec City in Canada, and had forced a British army and fleet out of Boston. By summer 1776, the revolutionary Congress, meeting in Philadelphia, had set up key components of national government such as an army and a currency.

Indeed one colony, Rhode Island, had already declared independence, on May 4, 1776. Over 90 separate declarations for independence had been issued by counties, towns, and legislatures. A month before the famous Declaration, Virginian congressional delegate Richard Henry Lee had introduced to Congress a resolution for separation.

A TALENT FOR COMPOSITION

On June 11, Congress tapped a committee of five—Adams, Thomas Jefferson of Virginia, Ben Franklin of Pennsylvania, New York's Robert Livingston, and Roger Sherman of Connecticut—to draft a document of independence. The wily, sometimes abrasive Adams picked Jefferson, hailing from the largest, most populous colony, as author. Adams told him: "You are a Virginian, and a Virginian ought to appear at the head of this business. Second, I am obnoxious, suspected, and unpopular. Third, you can write ten times better than I can."

Over 17 days, while beset like his fellow delegates with many pressing wartime tasks, the 33-year-old Jefferson put thoughts to parchment. Then he presented his draft to the committee, which made 47 mostly minor changes. Ben Franklin, a noted man of letters, likely altered the opening phrase, from, "We hold these truths to be sacred and undeniable" to "We hold these truths to be self-evident." The full Congress then deleted about a quarter of the text, including a rousing attack on the British slave trade, and a condemnation of the British people.

Jefferson, with his "happy talent of composition," drew heavily on source documents like his own preamble for Virginia's Constitution, Lee's resolution, and George Mason's Virginia Declaration of Rights, which later formed the basis of the Constitution's Bill of Rights. For instance, Mason had written, "That all men are by nature equally free and independent and have certain inherent rights . . . namely, the enjoyment of life and liberty . . . and pursuing and obtaining happiness." Jefferson was also influenced by English philosopher John Locke, with his notion of "natural rights" that no king could grant or rescind.

Powerful Preamble

The Declaration's introduction provides its rationale:

When in the Course of human events, it becomes necessary for one people to dissolve the political bands which have connected them with another, and to assume among the powers of the earth, the separate and equal station to which the Laws of Nature and of Nature's God entitle them, a decent respect to the opinions of mankind requires that they should declare the causes which impel them to the separation.

The preamble that follows has two parts. The first contains a famous call for universal freedom and equality, and an assertion of the democratic basis of authority:

We hold these truths to be self-evident, that all men are created equal, that they are endowed by their Creator with certain unalienable Rights, that among these are Life, Liberty and the pursuit of Happiness.

That to secure these rights, Governments are instituted among Men, deriving their just powers from the consent of the governed.

A LONG TRAIN OF ABUSES

The second part contains a people's "right of revolution":

When a long train of abuses and usurpations, pursuing invariably the same Object evinces a design to reduce them under absolute Despotism, it is their right, it is their duty, to throw off such Government.

The body of the text is a list of grievances against the British government and King George. Among the complaints, which illustrate the King's unfitness to rule, are: the suspension of trial by jury; the dissolution of legislatures; the cutting off of trade; and the many taxes—without representation in Parliament—which the British Crown had imposed. The Declaration blasts Britain's aggression: the King "has plundered our seas, ravaged our Coasts, burnt our towns, and destroyed the lives of our people," and has moved "large Armies of foreign Mercenaries"—German-speaking Hessians—"to compleat the works of death, desolation and tyranny."

SACRED HONORS

The declaration of separation follows:

We, therefore, the Representatives of the united States of America . . . do . . . solemnly publish and declare, That these United Colonies are, and of Right ought to be Free and Independent States.

Then a statement of powers that the new government should have:

They have full Power to levy War, conclude Peace, contract Alliances, establish Commerce, and to do all other Acts and Things . . .

Jefferson closed with a prayer-like oath by the delegates:

And for the support of this Declaration, with a firm reliance on the protection of divine Providence, we mutually pledge to each other our Lives, our Fortunes and our sacred Honor.

On July 4, 12 of the newly declared States approved the 1,337-word Declaration, and New York followed a week later.

Aftermath

The first to sign the Declaration was the President of Congress, John Hancock, who famously wrote his "John Hancock" in large letters. A story arose that Hancock did this to let King George see his name without putting on his reading glasses. Another anecdote emerged that Hancock, after the signing, stated that all the delegates "must now hang together," to which Ben Franklin replied: "Or most assuredly we shall all hang separately."

At first, the Declaration had a sharp, if limited, impact. When it was publicly read that July in towns throughout America, many crowds responded as they had in New York, where an equestrian statue of King George was pulled down and melted into bullets.

Over time, the Declaration's effect, especially its Preamble, was huge. Opponents of slavery contrasted its sweeping assertion of equality with the inequality of human ownership—notably so, President Lincoln, in his Gettysburg Address, when speaking of a "new nation . . . dedicated to the proposition that all men are created equal." A century later, advocates of liberty—from dissidents in the Soviet communist bloc to foes of South African apartheid—drew on the Declaration's lofty principles to build freer societies.

WALT DISNEY:
THEME PARKS AND FANTASY FILMS

All the experts called the three-year project his "Folly." He had to prescreen it for Bank of America to get the money to finish the thing. The price of the film, $1.5 million during the Great Depression, was colossal. But being a perfectionist cost money. He had to bring in expert advice to train his staff about special effects. Animators labored with his new invention, the multi-plane camera, which let illustrators change a character's movement against an unmoving background, saving countless hours of drawing. His studio also wrestled with names for the film's little "co-stars": Tubby, Puffy, Burpy, and Blabby were considered, and thankfully, dropped.

Adolescent Animator

But he was confident: he'd practiced his special gift from an early age. In the Missouri farm country where he grew up, he'd sketch pictures of a neighbor's horse. When the U.S. entered the First World War, he enlisted, at age 16, as an ambulance driver—and filled the windows of the car with cartoons.

When his Kansas City–based art studio failed in the early 1920s, he moved to Hollywood and started another studio with his brother Roy. Then his distributor slashed his fees, and pried away most of his animators. Undeterred, he began doodling out a new character. Since mistakenly killing an owl as a boy, he'd loved animals, and loved imagining them with human traits. He looked up from his drawing pad: he'd created Mickey Mouse.

With the help of his brother, his wife Lillian, and animator Ubbe Iwerks, Walt Disney put out brief movie cartoons of Mickey. He learned comic pacing from silent film great Charlie Chaplin, who also advised him on how to better protect his distribution rights. Competition was tough: other animators were putting out wildly popular characters like Popeye, Betty Boop, and Felix the Cat. But he became the first to synchronize sound with cartoon figures, and later created Technicolor. Yet his main inventions were his characters, like Donald Duck and Minnie Mouse. Audiences loved them, and the Three Little Pigs even more, with their hit song—"Who's Afraid of the Big Bad Wolf?"

So, with such a record of success and with such talent, he persevered with "Snow White and the Seven Dwarfs." After its release, it grossed $8 million, the highest gross for any movie in 1938.

Many feature-length animations followed, often adapted from European fairy tales: *Pinocchio,* for which Disney created Jiminy Cricket as a happy counter to the title character's misadventures. Also *Dumbo, Bambi, Cinderella, Peter Pan,* and *Sleeping Beauty,* among others—all box-office hits. A rare failure was *Fantasia,* set to the classical soundtrack of conductor Leopold Stokowski, yet now considered a classic. His movie work garnered an unsurpassed 59 Oscar nominations, and a record 27 awards.

Cinderella's Castles

In 1955, he invented the theme park, in part to have a safe place to entertain his two daughters. Disneyland, set in Anaheim, California, was populated with actors portraying his cartoon legends. The park was surrounded by a monorail, for he'd always loved railroads, and he actually built a miniature steam railroad, with a half mile of tracks, tunnel, and trestle, at his Los Angeles home.

Disneyland was so popular that Disney's company upped the ante. In 1971 it was to open Disney World, on a swath of land near Orlando, Florida that was twice the size of Manhattan. The theme park and hotel complex would include the Magic Kingdom, with iconic Cinderella's Castle, and the EPCOT Center, akin to a world's fair.

By then his company minions had dreamed up animatronics for the 1964 New York World's Fair, with a lifelike Abe Lincoln, and "It's a Small World After All," with lifelike children chanting the oh-so-catchy tune. They'd also pushed the boundaries of color photography on television, with *Walt Disney's Wonderful World of Color,* which inspired millions of kids to dream of joining the Mickey Mouse Club.

At the summit of his success, Walt Disney was felled by lung cancer, dying in 1966 at age 65. He left much of his considerable wealth to endow the new California Institute of the Arts (CalArts).

The Artiste of Fun

His company went on to manage Miramax Films and Touchstone Pictures, the American Broadcasting Company (ABC) and the

ABC Family Channel, and ESPN. But its influence had been greatest when Disney's creative genius roared from the 1930s to the mid-1960s, when America was at the heights of its own power and influence. Mickey Mouse, more than McDonald's, more than Elvis, might have been the most recognizable American name on the planet.

Like rock and roll and fast food, Walt Disney made Americana fun and accessible to all. Yet he also revolutionized the arts. A statement he made for CalArts, about classical composer Richard Wagner, could have applied to Disney himself:

"He conceived of a perfect and all-embracing art, combining music, drama, painting, and the dance . . . the vast orchestra of the art-in-combination."

FREDERICK DOUGLASS:
RIDE TO FREEDOM

The quiet, 20-year-old passenger on the northbound train out of Baltimore sat in a sailor's disguise, gripping fake identity papers. Tall, muscular, often sporting a mane of kinked hair brushed back from the forehead, he could transfix listeners with his eloquence. But on September 3, 1838, he was anxious to avoid attention, worried that several passengers had recognized him.

UNBROKEN BY SLAVERY

The impetus for his flight was clear. The son of a Maryland slave woman and, perhaps, her white overseer, Frederick Bailey had always known bondage. He grew up on the Wye Plantation in Maryland, where he and other shabbily dressed slave children scooped their small daily allotments of cornmeal out of a trough. Frederick had often witnessed public floggings. He'd been separated from his mother early in life and sent to live with his grandmother. The latter, when too old to work, was expelled from her cabin to die.

He battled back through self-education, offering bits of bread to white children in exchange for reading lessons. As a young teen, Frederick set up a Sunday school, and illegally taught reading to dozens of slaves. One Sunday, a mob of club-wielding plantation owners put an end to the lessons.

When Frederick was 16, his owner, Thomas Auld, sent him to Edward Covey, a farmer known for "breaking" uncooperative slaves. Covey whipped Frederick mercilessly. One day, as Covey tied him to the whipping post, Frederick fought back. "I seized Covey by the throat," recalled Frederick, "and as I did so, I rose." Covey finally ended the beating. Frederick concluded: "Men are whipped oftenest who are whipped easiest."

Auld then sent him to work for his Baltimore brother-in-law, Hugh Auld. Instead of field work, Frederick took on a skilled, paid job as a shipyard caulker. Still, he had to turn over most of his wages. And a gang of white workers beat Frederick up, badly injuring an eye. Hugh Auld was unable to take the men to court: the law forbade a jury from taking the word of a black man against a white.

RISING UP

Frederick joined the East Baltimore Mental Improvement Society. He poured over abolitionist writings. He also met Anna Murray, a free black servant woman. In 1838, they became engaged. Frederick resolved to flee to a free state, and have Anna follow. To this end he obtained the sailor's garb and false papers.

After a day and night of stealthy travel by train and steamboat, Frederick arrived in New York City a free man. "My gladness and joy," he wrote, "like the rainbow, defy the skill of pen or pencil."

Yet slave catchers prowled the streets to seize escaped blacks. So Frederick kept moving, to the whaling town of New Bedford, Massachusetts, where he found shipyard work. He was astonished at the efficiency of free labor, where a few eager workers with machines could do the work of many recalcitrant slaves. Still, the shipyards wouldn't hire blacks as skilled workers, and Frederick had to do the menial work of unloading cargo.

To hide his identity, Frederick Bailey changed his name to a character in a Walter Scott novel—and became Frederick Douglass. Meantime Anna joined him, and they married. Frederick and Anna Douglass would have five children.

An Abolitionist's Crusade

Douglass joined the movement to abolish slavery headed by New Englander William Lloyd Garrison. A natural storyteller, he was soon on speaking tours with Garrison, mesmerizing audiences with tales of his harsh plantation life. The lecture circuit had its dangers: an Indiana mob opposed to abolition assaulted Douglass, breaking his hand.

Douglass also had run-ins with Garrison and other abolitionists over the Constitution and the "back to Africa" movement. Garrison believed the founding document, with its "3/5ths of a man" voting rule for slaves, justified slavery, while Douglass thought it provided a path for its democratic abolition. Meantime some felt blacks should resettle in African nations like Liberia, while Douglass argued the true home of African Americans was America.

In 1845, despite the risk of drawing attention to himself, he published his memoir, *The Life and Times of Frederick Douglass*. It was a best-seller, and with the novel *Uncle Tom's Cabin*, became a bible of the abolitionists.

Partly to avoid slave catchers, he embarked on a speaking tour of Ireland and Britain. While abroad, two English friends purchased his freedom from the Auld family. The price: $710.96.

FREEING THE ENSLAVED

Back in America, Douglass moved to Rochester, New York. There he published a series of abolitionist newspapers, such as *The North Star*, despite calls from a New York paper to toss his printing press into Lake Ontario. When Rochester's public schools refused to admit his daughter Rosetta, Douglass successfully fought for their desegregation, anticipating nationwide school desegregation by a century.

He also attended, as the lone African American, the first women's suffrage conference, in Seneca Falls, New York. Yet he angered many supporters when he made Julia Griffiths, an English abolitionist, his business manager, and became her close companion. Garrison accused the two of engaging in an interracial, extramarital affair.

From their Rochester home, Frederick and Anna Douglass maintained one of the main stations on the Underground Railway, a network of homes and trails along which escaped slaves made their way to freedom. As many as ten fugitives at a time would bed down in the Douglass house.

Meantime the Civil War loomed. In 1859, John Brown—a leader of "free soil" forces fighting pro-slave bands in Kansas—plotted to ignite a slave revolt by seizing the Federal arsenal in Harpers Ferry, in present-day West Virginia. Brown wrote to Douglass, urging him to join the rebellion. While sympathetic, Douglass declined, believing an attack on Federal property would harm the anti-slavery cause.

After U.S. troops under Col. Robert E. Lee aborted Brown's uprising, letters between Douglass and Brown came to light. For his own safety, Douglass moved for a time to Canada.

Liaison with Lincoln

When war broke out in April, 1861, Douglass focused on persuading President Lincoln to free the slaves, and to allow blacks to fight for the Union.

For the latter, Douglass was an organizer for the famed "colored" regiment the 54th Massachusetts, depicted in the movie *Glory*. His pamphlets screamed: "Men of Color, to Arms!" His sons both served the cause, Lewis fighting in the unit, and Frederick, Jr., serving as a recruiter. However, Douglass's support for colored units cooled when the Union Army supplied blacks with inferior arms and denied them officer slots.

The freeing of the slaves came to pass with Lincoln's issuance in January 1863 of the Emancipation Proclamation. An emotional Douglass termed the decree an "answer to the agonizing prayers of centuries." In 1864, when the Union's military prospects seemed bleak, Lincoln asked Douglass to put together a plan to lead the slaves out of the Southern states, in the event of the North's defeat.

The war's successful conclusion brought three "freedom amendments" to the Constitution that seemed a culmination of Douglass's work. The 13th Amendment formally abolished slavery. The 14th Amendment guaranteed equal protection under the law to all Americans. And the 15th Amendment offered voting rights for all.

His work was hardly complete, however. Over time, due to fading interest in the North, and violence in the South from the Ku Klux Klan, the voting rights of Southern blacks and poor whites were eroded, and blacks were blocked from schools and jobs. Official segregation would last a hundred more years.

FIREBRAND TO THE END

In the postwar era, Douglass took on several prestigious posts, including Minister to Haiti, and U.S. Marshal for the District of Columbia. He also remained a friend of controversy. Some women's leaders like Susan B. Anthony berated him for giving priority to black suffrage over the right of females to vote. Douglass responded with the image of a racial lynching: "When women because they are women are dragged from their homes and hung upon lampposts . . . then they will have the urgency to obtain the ballot." After Anna Douglas died in 1882, Douglass married Helen Pitts, a white woman two decades his junior. Members of the Douglass and Pitts families disapproved of the interracial match.

Ironically, Douglass had mended fences with his former owner, Thomas Auld. In 1877, Douglass traveled to the plantation country where he'd grown up, and met the aged Auld. The two spoke at length, with the former master addressing the former slave as "Marshal Douglass." They reportedly parted amicably.

Douglass died in 1895, his handsome estate in the Anacostia district of Washington, D.C., destined to become a national historic site.

GEORGE EASTMAN:
INSTANT, EASY, AND CHEAP CREATION
OF PICTURES

In 2010–11, the entire Middle East was rocked by uprisings spread by images captured by cell-phone and other digital cameras and transmitted instantly to revolts in the same or adjoining lands. Nowadays, it's common to take instant digital and film photographs, and quickly transmit such photos and videos at little cost to friends and relations, or allies in a cause.

Yet, like many inventions taken for granted, portable, inexpensive photography is of recent origin. Until the 1880s, taking pictures was slow, cumbersome, and expensive. Photographers had to employ a large camera set on a heavy tripod, and laboriously develop in a darkened room costly and heavy photographic glass plates.

Industrious Dropout

By 1878, however, in Rochester, New York, this was destined to change. Maria Eastman would find her young son asleep many nights on the floor of the family dining room. George, a bank clerk by day, spent his nights experimenting with photographic processes, making use of the kitchen sink.

Young Eastman was an industrious boy from a hardworking yet hard-luck family. His sister died of polio at age 16. His father ran a Watertown, New York business school, but had to sell trees and flowers to make ends meet. At 14, Eastman himself dropped out of high school to earn money for his family.

He worked as an office boy for an insurance firm, and within a couple of years was writing policies. He got a higher-paying job as a bank clerk, but quit when someone less able got a prized promotion. He focused on his passionate hobby—photography—using money frugally saved from his work.

As he read every article on the subject, corresponded with other amateurs, and prepared his own photographic plates, Eastman knew well how tedious the "wet plate" process was. He wrote about "taking a very clean glass plate and coating it with a thin solution of egg white . . . Then we coated the plate with a solution of guncotton and alcohol mixed with bromide salts . . . the plate was dipped into a solution of nitrate of silver, the sensitizing agent in the dark."

So he was thrilled to read in the *British Journal of Photography* of a man working successfully with "dry plates," a potentially much cleaner, faster process, in which the plates could be stored for later use. Eastman set up a small dry plate shop above a Rochester music shop. He built a coating machine to rapidly turn out the plates. He optimistically bought a two-horsepower engine for the shop. "I really needed only a one-horsepower," the ambitious Eastman remembered. "I thought perhaps business would grow up to it."

Enthused, he brashly sailed to London, to the *Journal*'s office, and met its editor. He learned that the local dry plates business was hopelessly inefficient. So, back in America, Eastman patented his own approach. His plates began to sell briskly.

Later he took dry plates one better. With inventor William Hall Walker, he employed paper instead of glass as his template, and worked up a roller to easily insert the paper in the camera. Then with chemist Henry Reichenbach he devised a greater innovation, replacing paper with celluloid—a see-through, pliable material whose strips were rolled around a spindle within the camera.

A Box Camera in Every Home

In 1888, Eastman put out his "monster app": the Kodak, a portable, easy-to-use box camera, costing $25. The Kodak came with 100 exposures, which the owner shipped back to Eastman's Rochester factory for processing, and the camera then returned with prints and new film. "We were making photography an everyday affair," recalled Eastman. Even the Dalai Lama bought one.

Eastman was one of the first manufacturers to cheaply massmanufacture all the components of his product. By 1896, 100,000 Kodaks had been made, and each month a factory turned out 400 miles of photography paper. The price of a Kodak dropped to $5. Sales were boosted by a catchy ad: "You press the button, we do the rest."

In 1900, working with designer Frank Brownell, Eastman announced, for just $1, the Brownie, a wooden box camera, with an easily loaded roll of film. Forty exposures cost 30 cents. "We make the camera as convenient as the pencil," Eastman boasted. And a subject didn't have to sit still for a Brownie, which could catch a person or object in motion.

The Brownie heralded a great many other time- and labor-saving devices that the new century would bring, and in democratic, industrious America bring them to the great mass of people. And Eastman Kodak–style cameras, with many enhancements, would dominate their industry until the introduction—ironically, by Kodak, undercutting its own business—of digital cameras in the 1990s.

PHILANTHROPIC PHOTOGRAPHER

George Eastman went on to other creative work, in color photography, or "Kodachrome." But after establishing Eastman Kodak as a giant operation, philanthropy became his chief concern. His view of endowments was: "One can leave it for others to administer after he is dead. Or he can get it into action and have fun while he is still alive." He steered $100 million to the likes of the Tuskegee Institute, Rochester's Eastman School of Music, and especially to the Massachusetts Institute of Technology (MIT), which educated several top Eastman technologists.

Its grateful students composed the following verse to their unidentified benefactor, dubbed "Mr. Smith":

"Hurrah! Hurrah! for Tech and Boston beans,
Hurrah! Hurrah! for 'Smith,' who'er that means;
May he always have a hundred million in his jeans,
So we'll get—what we want—when we want it."

THOMAS ALVA EDISON
INVENTOR OF THE MODERN WORLD

The angry conductor peered into the baggage train, and at its 15-year-old occupant, a seller of candies for the Michigan-based railroad. One corner had a printing press for a railway newspaper, which the teenager ran on the side. Another had a small chemistry lab, another hobby of the youth. The lab had ignited a fire, whose smoke was filling the train's compartment. The conductor took the fellow by the ears and threw him off the train, along with his printing press and lab apparatus.

ENFANT TERRIBLE

Five years later, in 1867, the young man was working as a telegrapher for Western Union, and in his free time conducting experiments with lead batteries. One night, he spilled sulfuric acid, which seeped through the floor and onto the desk of his boss. He was fired.

Seven years later, "Al," as his family called him, devised a new kind of telegraph, the quadraplex, that simultaneously sent and received two telegrams in two directions. Western Union asked him how much he wanted for it. Al figured maybe $2,000, and asked the company what it was willing to pay. "Forty thousand" was the response, a huge sum for the time.

With this windfall, Thomas Alva Edison set up the world's first R&D lab, at Menlo Park, New Jersey. It had everything he and his assistants, ranging from mechanics to physicists, might need. "Eight thousand kinds of chemicals, every kind of screw made, every kind of cord or wire, various kinds of hoofs, shark's teeth, deer horns, tortoise shell . . . all ores." This "invention factory," hailed by some as Edison's greatest creation, proved the template for Silicon Valley and other centers of innovation.

MENLO'S WIZARD

At Menlo Park, Edison created an improved mouthpiece for Alexander Graham Bell's telephone, making the voice signals clearer and louder. He wondered if the human voice could be recorded. He rigged up a device that etched sound vibrations onto tinfoil. He tested it out with the words: "Mary had a little lamb." To his astonishment, the device played back his remark. He'd invented the phonograph. He joked: "I was always afraid of things that worked the first time."

Now world-famous, Edison found his next big endeavor harder to pull off. He pored over 40,000 pages of notes, and made 1,600 experiments with different materials, before finding one—a carbonized bamboo filament—that glowed steady and sure for 14 hours. Soon his lightbulbs lasted 1,200 hours. He shared credit for this world-shaking creation with his test supervisor, William J. Hammer.

With bulb in hand, Edison and his aides invented the system for generating and distributing electrical power, including generators, transmission lines, and switches. They built the first power station, in lower Manhattan, and supplied buildings with power and heat. The Vanderbilt family and J. P. Morgan bankrolled him, and by 1887, 121 Edison power plants stretched across America. "We will make electricity so cheap," he bragged, "that only the rich will burn candles."

Triumphs, Setbacks, and the Sweat of His Brow

Outgrowing Menlo Park, Edison's empire expanded into a huge new facility at West Orange, New Jersey, employing 10,000 workers. There, he noted, "I am experimenting upon an instrument which does for the Eye what the phonograph does for the Ear." This yielded, with the help of assistant William Dickson, the motion picture, and the movie camera—and another new industry. In all, Edison registered a record 1,093 patents.

He also invented catchphrases: "Genius is one percent inspiration and 99 percent perspiration." And "There is no substitute for hard work." But also: "I never did a day's work in my life. It was all fun."

He miscalculated at times. Edison wrongly guessed his phonograph was better suited for business dictation than listening pleasure. Competitors drove him and his motion picture camera out of the movie business. He fired Nikola Tesla, the inventor of alternating current, a transmitter of electrical power that is superior to the direct current Edison touted.

And success came with great effort. The Wizard of Menlo Park worked 16 hours at a stretch, napping where he could—sometimes on the company lawn. Tesla noted: "He had no amusement of any kind, and lived in utter disregard of the most elementary rules of hygiene." Some of that was untrue: Late at night in the lab, Edison would sit down at a pipe organ, and sing and down beer and sandwiches with colleagues. The one-time telegrapher also found time to have six children, nicknaming the first two Dot and Dash.

From an early age, Edison was largely deaf, yet even this he turned into an edge: "Deafness allowed me to work with less distraction and to sleep deeply, undisturbed."

When he died in 1931, the nation, now wired from coast to coast, dimmed its lights in respect.

ELLIS ISLAND:
IMMIGRANT EPICENTER

To the immigration officers of the late 1800s, it was an oft-repeated scene. Excited arrivals to New York's Ellis Island would hurry past a central pillar near the Registry Room, and reunite with family and friends who'd arrived in America before them. Czechs, Russians, Irish, Jews, Poles, Slovaks, and others rushed together and embraced. In myriad languages, presents were offered, the latest news of loved ones exchanged. Officials dubbed the pillar "the Kissing Post."

ENTRY EXAM

Newcomers to Ellis Island would disembark by the thousands from steamships run by firms like the Italian Steam Navigation

Company and the Cunard Line, to be ferried over to the island's immigration center. There, officials checked the arrivals to ensure they were healthy, crime-free, and eager to work.

Military surgeons with the U.S. Public Health Service performed brief physical exams. They also scrutinized immigrants for lameness, as they walked up a big staircase from the baggage area to the Great Hall. A physician would identify a person's ailment by placing a chalk mark on his clothing. "L" stood for lameness, "CT" for trachoma, "S" for senility. "X" meant a suspected mental defect, and a circled X meant a definite mental defect.

Immigrants were quizzed on where they were headed, how much money they had, whether they had a job lined up, and whether they had a criminal record. Wealthier immigrants, those traveling in first- and second-class aboard the ships, were afforded a big advantage. It was assumed they had sufficient means to support themselves, and faced less scrutiny than those traveling belowdecks in "steerage," or third class.

Contrary to general belief, authorities did not anglicize the foreign-sounding names of arrivals, but transcribed names from the steamship companies' manifests. The whole process of asking questions and checking paperwork and physical status lasted about four hours.

The Bureau of Immigration rejected about two percent of the arrivals. Among the reasons: contagious disease, mental insanity, or a likelihood of becoming indigent. Those refused admission had to take a ship back home. This could be heart-wrenching, especially when families had to decide whether to split up.

MASS MIGRATIONS

New York City had long been the nation's busiest immigrant entry point. Before Ellis Island, there was the state-run Castle Garden in the Battery, on the south end of Manhattan. Castle Garden processed, from 1855 to 1890, some eight million arrivals, many from famine-stricken Ireland, or revolution-torn Germany. But con men would trawl the crowds of immigrants, often raking in their scarce funds for bogus jobs or fake railroad tickets. To make immigration safer and more efficient, and handle the huge numbers, the federal government set up a new offshore center.

The first Ellis Island immigrant, processed on January 1, 1892, was 15-year-old Annie Moore, of Cork, Ireland. She was reunited with her parents, who'd arrived in America before her; the Superintendent of Immigration handed the girl a ten-dollar gold piece. Other, later arrivals became famous, such as comedian Bob Hope, helicopter inventor Igor Sikorsky, "God Bless America" composer Irving Berlin, and Frank Capra, the Sicilian-born director of iconic American films like *It's a Wonderful Life.*

The number of immigrants at Ellis Island peaked in 1907 at 1.25 million; 11,747 arrived on that year's busiest day. From 1892 to 1924, 12 million new Americans stepped through the island's gates. It is estimated that 100 million Americans, a third of the country's population, are their descendants. Between Ellis Island and Castle Garden, from the mid-1800s to the early 1900s, about 25 million immigrants entered America. It was the greatest mass migration in human history.

THE FLOOD WATERS RECEDE

After the First World War, fears of revolutions abroad merged with concern over the rising numbers of foreign-born Americans. As a result, Congress in 1921 and 1924 passed strict immigration quotas. Ellis Island became something of a backwater—a holding area for suspected foreign radicals in 1918–19, and for suspected enemy aliens during the Second World War, as well as a temporary residence for refugees.

The immigration center was made into an Immigration Museum in 1990, after Chrysler Corp. Chairman Lee Iacocca led a private effort to restore the center and the nearby Statue of Liberty. By 2001, museum visitors could look their ancestors up in a database holding Ellis Island's 22 million immigration records. Or, on the museum's Wall of Honor, they can proudly inscribe the name of an immigrant forebear, such as the author's Celtic grandmother, one Bridget McGonigle.

A FEDERAL BANK:
TO BE OR NOT TO BE

The United States was broke. Holders of mortgage and other land-related debt were in hock to foreign lenders. Wars had put the country deeply in the red. The economy, some thought, would stagger or even collapse from the weight of so much borrowing. The federal bank, some argued, had to in effect bail the country out.

America in 2011? No, America at its founding. Indeed, disputes over public borrowing, and a central federal bank to lend the funds, have occurred since the very start of the United States.

NATIONAL BANK NUMBER 1

In 1791, the first federal Administration, George Washington's, set up the First Bank of the United States. It was actually a government-supported private bank that did some public business. It collected and deposited federal excise tax revenues and made loans to the new government and other borrowers. The Bank was part of Treasury Secretary Alexander Hamilton's plan—along with paying off the $54 million national debt from the Revolutionary War, and setting up a new national currency to supplant the 50 different currencies then in circulation—to establish the financial credit of the United States.

The Bank was controversial from the start. Speaker of the House James Madison and Secretary of State Thomas Jefferson, both Virginians, opposed it. They argued the Constitution didn't allow it, that it was geared to Northern interests, and that, by mixing public and private money, it would foster corruption. President Washington, with hesitation, signed the Bank into law. Hamilton initially financed it through a sleight of hand, by which the government borrowed against the Bank with funds it did not yet have. But the Bank, like his plan overall, for the most part worked.

The Bank was limited to an initial 20-year charter. In 1811, when its term was up, Madison, by then President, let its charter expire. Partly due to the lack of a national bank, the U.S. had much trouble financing the War of 1812. By its end, Philadelphia financier Stephen Girard, who'd acquired most of the assets of the First Bank, was single-handedly propping up the government's war debt.

NATIONAL BANK NUMBER 2

So, in 1816, President Madison approved the Second Bank of the United States. Like the prior Bank, it was largely a private entity. The government provided one fifth of its initial $35 million in funds ($550 million in 2010 dollars). Private-sector shareholders picked 15 of its board members, and the President the rest. Its charter was also limited to 20 years.

The Second Bank ran into trouble partly due to the aftermath of the War of 1812, which took place during Europe's devastating Napoleonic wars. During its postwar recovery, Europe bought much U.S. produce, helping touch off a U.S. economic boom. In 1819, to cool off an overheating economy, the Bank began calling in some of its loans. It called in further loans to make $4 million in payments due on money borrowed for the 1803 Louisiana Purchase. The resulting recession angered many businesses as well as debt holders, including War of 1812 hero Gen. Andrew Jackson. Meantime, the Bank's Baltimore branch was caught stealing $1 million in funds. Some states began taxing Bank branches, until Chief Justice John Marshall's Supreme Court in 1819 ruled such actions unconstitutional.

For a time, the Bank was on more solid ground, after President James Monroe appointed the brilliant if headstrong Philadelphian Nelson Biddle to serve as its head. Biddle had entered Princeton at age 10, and by age 20 had audited the books of the Louisiana Purchase. Yet trouble returned in 1831, when Biddle's brother Thomas and a congressman killed each other in a duel after arguing over Nelson Biddle's Bank policies. The following year, the newly appointed President Andrew Jackson vetoed a bill to renew the charter of the Bank, which he viewed as a potential monopoly. Jackson then won re-election, despite massive contributions from banks for his opponent, Kentucky Sen. Henry Clay.

In 1833, Jackson fired two of his Treasury Secretaries who refused to move the Bank's deposits to state banks, until Treasury Secretary Roger Taney, Jackson's future Chief Justice nominee, finally did. An angry Biddle then cut back on the Bank's lending, helping spark a recession. Mobs enraged by the economic downturn threatened Biddle's life. The wild "Bank War" ended in 1836, when Congress declined to renew the Bank's charter. Then came the financial Panic of 1837, caused in part by the termination of the Bank. Biddle resigned his post, was charged with fraud, was acquitted, then died a broken man.

National Bank Number 3

The U.S. had no national bank from 1836 until the early twentieth century, a time of generally rapid growth. Then some federal officials became concerned about the country's ability to respond to financial crises. Major financial panics had taken place in 1893, and in 1907, when banking magnate J. P. Morgan had to personally intervene to head off an economic crash.

After the panic, Congress appointed a National Monetary Commission, led by Vermont Sen. Nelson Aldrich. Chairman of the Senate Finance Committee, Aldrich was known as "General Manager of the Nation," as the country's leading authority on taxes and banks. (His grandson was President Gerald Ford's Vice President, Nelson Aldrich Rockefeller.) Aldrich led a mission to Europe to study its central banks.

Sen. Aldrich was influenced by prominent New York banker Paul Warburg, author of *A Plan for a Modified Central Bank*. Under the ruse of a duck hunting trip to Jekyll Island, Georgia, in 1910, Sen. Aldrich met with Warburg, with a partner of Morgan's, and with other influential bankers and academics. They concluded that, to efficiently smooth out financial excesses, the U.S. government needed its own central bank.

In 1913, based on Aldrich's recommendations, and after congressional approval, President Woodrow Wilson set up the Federal Reserve. The Federal Reserve consists of 12 branch banks around the country; a Federal Open Market Committee to regulate monetary policy, that is, its supply of money, often through interest rates; and a seven-person management Federal Reserve Board, including a Chairman and Vice Chairman, nominated by the President, with congressional approval. The Fed was charged with trying to keep the financial system stable and later, to try to keep prices and unemployment low.

FIGHTS OVER THE FED

In recent decades, as its influence has grown, the Fed has been in the thick of controversial issues. In the 1980s, critics said it slowed down the economy too much to fight inflation by keeping money too tight. In the late 1990s, some accused it of not foreseeing the "dot. com" Internet bubble whose bursting slowed the economy. Then, in the aftermath of the burst bubble and the 9-11 terror attacks, when it tried to head off a more severe recession, the Fed was criticized of overstimulating the economy and mortgage banks. Its actions took on huge proportions during the financial collapse of 2008, as it made $9 trillion in steeply discounted, overnight loans to Wall Street companies and major banks.

As in the early days of the United States, the future role of a central federal bank will likely remain contentious.

FOOD IN THE U.S.A.:
AS AMERICAN AS AVOCADO PIZZA

It's sometimes humorously noted that, if the United States lost the Second, or First, World War, then "we'd be speaking German today." But an even worse fate might have ensued if America lost its American Revolution to the British. Today we might be eating bangers and chips, and drinking warm beer.

American cuisine began with the seeming intent of keeping the traditionally bland British approach to food. That notion was immediately undermined by Native Americans, African arrivals, and savory-seeking Southerners, and has been under siege ever since by omni-devouring arrivals from throughout the world.

NATIVE VITTLES

The interaction of Europeans and American Indians sparked perhaps the greatest food exchange in history. The Indians brought to the table many native fruits—tomatoes, potatoes, squash, grapes, blueberries, and apples—many kinds of beans, many nuts, including peanuts, and what became the American staple crop of corn. The English brought boiled vegetables and meats, including lamb and pork, and baked meats, breads, puddings, and pies.

From their first Thanksgivings on, New Englanders embraced local plants and animals to yield roasted turkey, lobster bisque, clam chowder, cranberry sauce, and clam bakes. The British love of roasts thrived on a continent whose broad prairies, corn and wheat fields, and extensive ranches were to supply nearly limitless grain feed and cattle. A wealthy nation provided sufficient income to purchase much meat, including steaks, which were luxuries elsewhere, while in the U.S. a "meat and potatoes" diet became commonplace.

SOUTHERN FRIED

In the South, Africans brought in or developed a love of healthy, boiled vegetables like okra, black-eyed peas, and turnip and collard greens. They, like the Scotch-Irish in the upcountry, and the English planters in the lowlands, feasted on corn grits, biscuits, corn bread, and griddle cakes. The English cavaliers brought a taste for elegant cuisine. In France and Italy, diplomat Thomas Jefferson bought up innumerable local seeds, then tried them out at Monticello, to see what thrived, or died, on American soil.

In Virginia, pigs were omnipresent, and in addition to succulent ham, Southern favorites incorporated practically every part of the pig, including the intestines, or chit'lins, and even the brains and feet. Fried foods were cherished, like pork rinds, fried chicken, and chicken fried steak. At a time when supplies of fresh potable water were scarce, grain alcohol was a chief beverage in early America, consumed at an annual average of seven gallons a man. At Kentucky distilleries, whiskey gave way to corn-bred bourbon.

A succulent Southern confection that grew into an all-American tradition was barbecue, influenced by slaves making smoked meats marinated with spices. Made from pig plied with vinegary sauce in the Carolinas, and sweet tomato sauce further south, barbecue is cooked over hickory wood in Tennessee. In Texas, barbecued meat is chunky beef, dispensed originally from the chuck wagons of cattle drives.

From the start, culinary heaven was New Orleans, with its gumbo stew of Spanish, French, Afro-Caribbean, and American-Indian flavors, refined French Creole and earthy Cajun menus, and regional standouts like jambalaya, blackened bayou catch, and the impossibly-stuffed mufaletta sandwich.

Northern Noshing, Southwestern Snacking

An early wave of European immigrants, the Irish, brought a taste for cabbage, potatoes, and boiled meats that was bland and British-like. But the Germans, America's largest immigrant group after the English, more than atoned for that Puritan palate. Spreading across fertile tracts of Pennsylvania, and the upper Midwest, they brought wursts and grilled classic American food named for Old World towns: the Hamburg-er, and the Frankfurt-er, both often served with the French staple of deep-fried potatoes. Such heavy fare was reinforced by the immigrant Poles, with their kielbasas. In Milwaukee and St. Louis, Germans dominated the beer industry, though their New World brew tasted watery to Old World tastes. That inadequacy was fixed generations later with the appearance of microbreweries making sharp-tasting pilsners and hearty ales.

The 1848 annexation of the Southwest brought in a flood of Mexican cuisine, including flatbreads, chilies, spices, rice, and many beans, refried pinto and others. By the late 20th century, as the population of Hispanics mushroomed, burritos became as popular as burgers, and salsa and chips as common an appetizer as cheese and crackers.

FUN FOODS

The explosion of immigration around 1900 from south Italy brought along more "all-American" cuisine: spaghetti and meatballs, and other pastas, and what is likely today's most popular American food, pizza—hand-tossed in New York, deep-dished in Chicago, improbably fruity in California. Jewish arrivals brought the now-ubiquitous bagel, once austerely served plain or lightly seeded, its flour now heretically mixed at times with blueberries and other fruit.

Americans were intent in their culinary pursuit of happiness, as evidenced in the late 1800s and early 1900s, by the creation of enduring "fun foods," such as salt-water taffy, Jell-O, malted shakes, Oreo cookies, peanut butter and jelly sandwiches, popsicles, Kool-Aid, and Twinkies. The 1904 World's Fair in St. Louis introduced the ice cream cone to a wide audience. Potato chips, first devised in the 1850s in Saratoga Springs, New York for ship and railway tycoon Cornelius Vanderbilt, were mass-produced by Herman Lay in the 1920s.

A somewhat healthier development was the peculiar American practice of having cereal for breakfast. Cereal was created originally as a hospital food by the Kellogg brothers of Battle Creek, Michigan. Somewhere in the middle of the health spectrum were "tonics" like Coca Cola, concocted in 1886 by Atlanta pharmacist Dr. John Pemberton, and served from the soda fountains of pharmacies.

High-Tech Tastes

At the same time, technology was revolutionizing food, mass-producing and mass-processing it, often canning it. With the invention of refrigerated railroad cars, frozen foods became available nationwide in every season. An important innovation occurred in 1923, when taxidermist Clarence Birdseye devised a way to quick-freeze and fast-pack vegetables. Such innovations were also to make possible some arguably less delectable products like TV dinners.

Frozen patties and mechanical mixers, plus assembly-line efficiency, gave McDonald's Ray Kroc and his many imitators the chance to make "fast food" into vast franchise outlets. This fulfilled a long trend of offering inexpensive fare in easily accessible venues, like roadside taverns, diners, and cafeterias, for a restless, fast-moving, rapidly consuming people.

The easy availability and cheap price of all these foodstuffs, along with the automation of much work and transport, produced a uniquely American problem—an epidemic of obesity. By 2007, the United States was the most overweight affluent nation. The incidence of both diabetes and heart disease was marked. A cottage industry of diets, and diet books, sprung up, as did vast networks of gyms, and Red Bull and Gatorade energy drinks. The growing standardization and processing of food produced a reaction in the form, by the 1970s, of a back-to-basics binge, of health food, and of organic farms.

C.I.A. Cookery

Tastes of all kinds kept expanding. A factor was the Second World War, which exposed millions to exotic climes and cuisines. A major player here was Julia Child, who served with the CIA precursor the Office of Strategic Services in China, where she gleaned intelligence on Szechuan and Cantonese cookery, destined for great things back in the States. She also married Foreign Service Officer Paul Child, a gourmand who exposed her to the sophistication of continental cuisine, which she introduced to the public with the book *Mastering the Art of French Cooking*, and with long-running television shows. When the Smithsonian's American History museum recently opened an exhibit on Child, tourists abandoned Lincoln's stovepipe hat, Dorothy's Wizard of Oz ruby slippers, and Elvis Presley's guitar to swarm about her kitchen instead.

The immigration in recent decades of many non-Europeans has brought in "exotic" feasts. Chinese food, introduced to America during the 1849 California Gold Rush, and thence trickling into Chinatowns scattered around America, became a standard neighborhood or mall offering. Also becoming ubiquitious were East Indian restaurants, which popularized lentils, yogurt, turmeric. Some of the newer arrivals were refugees from foreign trouble spots, such as the Vietnamese who, in fleeing their 1970s-era war-torn home, brought along spring rolls, and pho noodle soup, which is similar to chicken soup, a reviving folk remedy for the common cold. Washington, D.C., saw entire city blocks taken over by restaurants run by Ethiopians, who introduced the novel custom of eating with one's *thoroughly-washed* hands.

By the early twenty-first century, the nation's insatiable appetite had digested the entire world.

HENRY FORD:
PERSONAL TRANSPORT FOR ALL

In 1908, the Ford Motor Company was a prosperous and ongoing concern. One of the 80 or so car makers in America, it was churning out 100 vehicles a day, and netting a tidy profit. It had even sponsored a race car that, at 91.3 mph, set the world's speed record.

But its largest shareholder, Henry Ford, wasn't satisfied. "I will build a motor car for the great multitude," he stated. To lower prices and hike sales, he wanted to turn out a thousand cars a day.

His fellow shareholders—including his parts and chassis suppliers, the Dodge brothers, Horace and John—were aghast. More volume meant lower prices and, they feared, fewer dividends. They took Ford to court.

YOUTHFUL TINKERER

Born in Dearborn, Michigan, in 1863 to Irish farmers fleeing the potato famine, Ford was a mechanical genius impatient with the status quo. He spent a good part of his teens pulling apart and re-assembling pocket watches. On his parents' farm he built a steam-powered tractor.

In 1885, the German Karl Benz had invented the gasoline-powered car. Ford, while chief engineer for the Edison Illuminating Company in Detroit, spent off hours building his own cars. His first was a four-horsepower "Quadricycle" mounted atop bicycle wheels. In 1899 he founded the Henry Ford Company, which became Cadillac Motor when Ford quit after a spat with financiers.

Later, at Ford Motor Company, he lost his court case with the Dodge brothers, then bought them out. With complete control of the firm, he rolled out his dream car—the Model T.

A GRAND CARRIAGE FOR THE COMMON MAN

Until then, most cars were handcrafted, and geared to the wealthy. The Model T was aimed at the average Joe—it was durable, simple in design, easy to fix. Its price, $950 at first, fell in 1927 to a cut-rate $290: $3,580 in 2010 dollars.

The plunging price was due to Ford's borrowing of ideas on rapid manufacture from the likes of camera maker George Eastman. Workers would quickly piece together streams of incoming components on moving assembly lines. Production time for a chassis was slashed from 728 to 93 minutes.

"Nothing is particularly hard," said Ford, "if you divide it into small jobs."

Building the cars, by 1914, were employees collecting $5 a day, compared to $2.34 for the average industrial worker. Ford figured his "wage motive" gave more money to those most likely to buy his cars. The high salaries also encouraged loyalty: previously, many slots at Ford had turned over four times a year. Afterwards, skilled mechanics vied to work at Ford, which also broke ground through eight-hour shifts and 40-hour weeks.

The World on Wheels

The work was done at huge production plants in Michigan's Highland Park, then River Rouge, the latter the world's biggest factory. Over time, to feed these beasts, Ford acquired his own coal mines, forests, glassworks, and freighters.

By 1927, almost 17 million Model Ts had been purchased worldwide, half the world's output. Forty-five years passed before this sales mark was broken. To boost sales further, Ford set up franchises in every U.S. city, and plants in India, Brazil, even Stalin's Russia.

He boasted: "The horse is DONE."

Henry Ford's stubborn persistence made his company number one but also undermined its success. For 19 years, the Model T hardly changed, while competitors rolled out yearly models with innovations like six-cylinder engines, hydraulic brakes, and choice of color. ("People can have the Model T in any colour," Ford had remarked, "so long as it's black.") By the mid-1930s, the company dropped to third place behind General Motors and Chrysler.

Yet by then, Ford's assembly lines and inexpensive cars had radically changed the country. Asphalt roads, motels, and suburbs sprouted in and around America's cities. The nation—from formerly isolated farmers to restless teens to newly mechanized teamsters—now held the liberating keys to the road.

A company ad stated: "Every day is 'Independence Day' to him who owns a Ford."

ROBERT FULTON:
FROM ANCIENT SAIL TO MODERN STEAM

Hoots and catcalls rang out from the thousands peering from Manhattan's shoreline in August 1807, as the strange-looking ship pulled out onto its maiden voyage. The 142-foot-vessel had masts and canvas like a sailboat, but a large funnel that threw out smoke and sparks, and circular paddle wheels. On the deck, the *Clermont*'s tall, curly-haired architect remained resolute, even as onlookers yelled out: "Fulton's Folly!"

THE SKIPPER OF THE NAUTILUS

Forty-one-year-old Robert Fulton had had his share of setbacks. In 1803, while demonstrating a prototype of his steam-powered boat to the French, the ship had broken in half and sunk in the Seine. He'd turned to another creation, the *Nautilus,* a 20-foot-long "plunging boat" that could stay submerged for an hour, its four-man crew breathing super-compressed air. In a test before Britain's Royal Navy, a floating mine from the submarine blew up a 200-ton brig. But the British, afraid of the threat to their maritime mastery, had offered Fulton hush money to keep his creation a secret.

Raised in Lancaster, Pennsylvania, Fulton was inventive from the start, building a foot-powered paddle wheel for his boyhood pals, and nicknamed "Quicksilver Bob" for devising Fourth of July rockets. A skilled drawer, he painted the elderly Ben Franklin in miniature, then moved to London, where he was the protégé of artist Benjamin West, head of the Royal Academy. Fulton also worked for the appropriately named Earl of Bridgewater, sponsor of one of the first canals. The American invented a mechanical plane for lifting and lowering canal barges.

In France in 1802, Fulton met New York financier Robert Livingston in Paris to negotiate the Louisiana Purchase. Livingston agreed to bankroll Fulton's steamboat dreams, and secured him a long-term monopoly on Hudson River traffic. This gave Fulton an advantage over rival inventors like John Fitch, who was making short, steam-powered voyages out of Philadelphia.

Fulton oversaw the *Clermont*'s construction, outfitting it with a 24-horsepower steam engine procured from Boulton & Watt, the company cofounded by James Watt, the steam engine's inventor.

A MARVELOUS MAIDEN VOYAGE

With the Clermont's launch, the jeers on Manhattan's shore turned to plaudits. Fulton's ship chugged upriver at four to five miles an hour, for 150 miles, reaching its destination of Albany, New York, in 32 hours. For $7 a fare, Fulton ran regular trips between the two cities, the world's first successful commercial steamship line. Sailing vessels dependent on the vagaries of wind couldn't compete.

The great inventor had finally achieved success, but tragedy intervened. During the War of 1812, the U.S. Navy commissioned Fulton to make a steam-powered, 120-horsepower warship. He wore himself out working outdoors on the project in the bitter winter of 1814. One day, walking with colleagues on the frozen Hudson, a friend fell through the ice. Fulton jumped in, saving him, but caught pneumonia. He died on February 24, 1815, leaving behind four children and wife Harriet Livingston Fulton.

Still, his ideas were wildly popular. By 1827, 200 steamboats were plying America's rivers and coasts, sparking a great economic boom, while slashing travel time between the growing nation's disparate regions.

The Wild Battle of
Gettysburg:
A Turning Point

The Union was on the verge of breaking up, the South on the verge of successful secession.

On July 2, 1863, the second day of the Battle of Gettysburg, in the rolling hills of southern Pennsylvania, the Confederate Army had just about turned the Union army's left flank. If it did take the heights, of Devil's Den, and Little Round Top, and got into the Northern forces' rear, it could roll up the whole opposing army. If it did, it might then move to seize the capital of Washington, and end the war.

At 6 p.m. that sweltering day, the Union regiment on Devil's Den was much outnumbered by a brigade of Southerners, part of a powerful corps commanded by Gen. James Longstreet. In desperation, the Northern commander ordered his men to fix bayonets, and charge. The gambit worked, the high ground was held.

On the adjacent rise, the Confederate troops under Texan Gen. John Bell Hood neared the summit. They were terribly thirsty from maneuvering for hours in the heat and famished from their meager rations of corn. The Union defenders, under Maine Col. Joshua Chamberlain, were in worse straits: they were out of ammunition. In desperation, Chamberlain ordered his troops to charge with bayonets. Again the tactic worked, and the hill was held.

For three days, the epic fight, the bloodiest of the Civil War, went that way, see-sawing, a game of inches, victory and defeat within both sides' grasp multiple times.

The Fog of War

It started by chance. The South's 72,000-strong Army of Northern Virginia, commanded by Virginian Robert E. Lee, the Federal Army's former chief of staff, had invaded the North. It hoped to defeat the Union's 94,000-strong Army of the Potomac. It was confident, with Lee having recently trounced the North in major battles at Fredericksburg and Chancellorsville. The Northern army's commander, meanwhile, was untested: President Lincoln had appointed Major Gen. George Meade three days before Gettysburg commenced.

The lead unit for the Confederates, badly short of supplies such as boots, headed toward the town of Gettysburg in search of shoes. The local Union commander, veteran Indian fighter Brig. Gen. John Buford, realized that a line of ridges, stretching in a fishhook pattern from northeast to southwest, from Culp's Hill to Little Round Top, offered ground to make a stand.

Buford was superseded by Maj. Gen. Winfield S. Hancock, who

agreed with the line of defense, stating: "I think this the strongest position by nature upon which to fight a battle."

Before the Union could fully get its army into position, powerful Confederate forces arrived, beating up two Northern corps, ending the battle's first day. The South had a chance to occupy the town of Gettysburg, but the attack's leader, Lt. Gen. Richard Ewell, perhaps somewhat hesitant from having lost a leg in a previous fight, lost the chance.

Day two brought the near capture of the two Union hills. The assault on Little Round Top itself came about by chance, when Union Gen. Dan Sickles, ignoring orders, advanced at the Peach Orchard into the Confederate advance, touching off a fierce fight, and diverting the rebels into the rise. The Southern assault there was little helped by a diversionary attack to the north by Ewell on Culp's Hill. Much delayed until 7 p.m., it was repulsed.

On day three, July 3, Lee determined to repeat the attempt that nearly worked the previous day, and attack the Union left, with a simultaneous supporting assault on Culp's Hill. But again chance intervened, when a surprise Union cannonade touched off a fight for the hill well before the main attack was ready.

A FATEFUL CHARGE

Fatefully, fatally, Lee switched plans, to charge the Union center. He rejected the strong advice of Longstreet, who preferred a flank attack, as at Chancellorsville, or staying on the defensive, as at Fredericksburg. Lee believed the Union's middle had been hollowed to defend its flanks, and the North obliged this notion by holding fire when the South began pounding its center with the war's largest artillery barrage, from 160 guns. The cannonade did little damage to the Union lines, well-fortified by the tenacious Meade, who benefitted from another Southern shortage: cannon shells.

Confederate Maj. Gen. George Pickett had meantime arrived with a fresh division of infantry. His "Pickett's Charge," of over 12,000 soldiers, took place across 1,200 yards of open ground and took a devastating Union fire of rifles, 70 cannons, and canister shot, cutting a swath through the masses of men. The attack grazed against the Union front at "Bloody Angle." Americans fought hand to hand with Americans; some had served together in the Federal army. One, Confederate Brig. Gen. Lewis Armistead, fell mortally wounded at a spot defended by his friend Union Gen. Hancock, as depicted in the film *Gettysburg*. Meade funneled in reinforcements, ending the assault. Barely half of Pickett's men made it back to their lines.

POSTMORTEM

Mauled, the South fell back to its own line of defensive ridges. "It's all my fault," murmured Lee, who may have suffered from a heart murmur at the time. Here chance again played a role, as heavy rains fell on July 4, Independence Day, for the North. Lee took the opportunity to retreat southward under cover of mist, and Meade, to Lincoln's dismay, decided to not to risk further battle. Casualties on both sides were about even, and horrific—about 23,000 killed, wounded, missing, or captured for each.

That same day, the town of Vicksburg, Mississippi, key to the control of the Mississippi, and the South's supply lines, fell after a long siege to Union Gen. Ulysses S. Grant. Nine days later, riots over the military draft broke out in New York City, but the triumph at Gettysburg made their effect bearable to the Union instead of possibly decisive against it.

Gettysburg meant the South would never mount another major invasion of the North, which would inexorably grind its way to victory. European powers considering intervention on the Southern side decided to sit it out. It was thus the turning point of the war, and of a nation's history.

Robert Goddard:
Rocket Man

It was a public humiliation for the country's first rocket scientist.
In 1920, Robert Goddard, a 32-year-old professor at Clark
University in Massachusetts, had published a scientific paper, "A
Method for Reaching Extreme Altitudes." His paper stated that a
rocket could not only travel in the vacuum of space, but could reach
the Moon. Citing Isaac Newton, the editorial board of *The New York
Times* scoffed: "That professor Goddard, with his 'chair' in Clark
College . . . does not know the relation of action to reaction; and of
the need to have something better than a vacuum against which to
react . . . he only seems to lack the knowledge ladled out daily in high
schools."

DREAMING OF THE STARS

Actually, in lab experiments performed five years prior, Goddard had demonstrated that rockets could move in a vacuum and, thus, in the airlessness of outer space. Born in Massachusetts, Goddard had long dreamt of such things. At 17, after clambering up a cherry tree, he'd gazed into an idyllic New England autumn sky and wondered how to traverse it. "I imagined how wonderful it would be to make some device which had even the possibility of ascending to Mars," he recalled. "I was a different boy when I descended the tree . . . for existence at last seemed very purposive."

As a student at Worcester Polytechnic Institute, he put his ideas to metal, firing off a test rocket in a school cellar, filling it with gunpowder smoke. Luckily, the faculty indulged him, including his instructor, a founder of the American Physical Society. Goddard earned his Ph.D., was appointed an Institute teacher, and by 1914 held patents for three breakthrough technologies: liquid-fueled rockets, as in hydrogen fuel; solid-fueled rockets, as in liquid oxygen; and multi-stage rockets. All would become standard issue during the Space Age.

When the First World War erupted, Goddard invented the rudiments of the bazooka. In place of gunpowder, he used dynamite and nitroglycerine, with the weapon handheld, or fired from a makeshift rack.

A GENIUS SHUNNED

The 1920s brought more successes, and setbacks. On March 16, 1926, in an experiment at the Auburn, Massachusetts farm of his Aunt Effie, Goddard launched the first liquid-fueled missile. Lit with a blowtorch, the thin, 10-foot-tall missile reached a height of 41 feet in its 2.5-second flight, before thudding into a cabbage patch. In 1929, Goddard launched the first rocket with scientific instruments, a barometer and camera. He paid for these experiments out of his own pocket and with funds from the Smithsonian.

Another launch in Auburn generated a loud roar and fiery flash that convinced neighbors an airplane had crashed. Two police ambulances vainly searched for survivors; the area's newspaper printed a mocking headline: "Moon Rocket Misses Target by 238,799-½ Miles!" Besieged by citizen complaints, the town's fire marshal told Goddard to take his tests elsewhere.

Blasting to Success

With a $100,000 pledge from philanthropist Harry Guggenheim, Goddard and a small team of scientists in 1930 moved their operation to Roswell, New Mexico, later famous for misinterpreting aircraft as UFOs. Over the next nine years, under the Southwest's clear skies, Goddard conducted 48 tests, broke the sound barrier, and reached altitudes of 9,000 feet. He also built the first rockets with gyroscopic controls. In all, the scientist received 214 patents, and won a $1 million settlement from the U.S. government for patent infringement.

In the Second World War, he worked for the Navy, specializing in jet propulsion. He made progress in developing liquid-propellant motors and jet-assisted flight. As the conflict ended, Goddard died at age 57.

The war, meantime, had proven the value of his ideas. German scientists applied many of his brainstorms to their long-range V-2 rockets, missiles that destroyed much of London. One captured Nazi engineer, asked about the technology's origins, replied: "Why don't you ask your own Dr. Goddard? He knows better than any of us."

Goddard's own country acknowledged his genius in 1959, when NASA established the Goddard Space Flight Center. The Center helped plan the first manned mission to the Moon in 1969.

That year, *The New York Times* issued a belated apology for its putdown of Goddard a half century before: "It is now definitely established," the newspaper stated, "that a rocket can function in a vacuum as well as in an atmosphere. The *Times* regrets the error."

As the nation's first rocket scientist himself put it: "Every vision is a joke until the first man accomplishes it; once realized, it becomes commonplace."

THE GOLD RUSH CREATES THE GOLDEN STATE

California was a backwater. Once a province of Mexico, and by 1846, with the Mexican-American war, loosely under U.S. military control, it had perhaps 8,000 Spanish inhabitants, and roughly a thousand Americans. Far greater in number were the Native Americans inhabiting the Sierra Nevadan foothills. The population of Yerba Buena, soon to be renamed San Francisco, was 600.

GOLD FEVER!

One of the few prominent Americans was John Augustus Sutter, whom the Mexicans had granted 39,000 acres to keep out bandits,

Indians—and Americans. Across the Sierra at the American River, about 250 miles east of San Francisco, Sutter built an 18-foot-high adobe fort. He hired another American, James Marshal, to operate a sawmill there. On January 24, 1848, Marshal noticed gold in the mill water. Sutter swore him to secrecy, but word got out. Mormons and Indians soon discovered other mother lodes.

Wily San Francisco merchant Sam Brannan bought up all the mining supplies in town. On May 12, he paraded through the streets hoisting a bottle of gold dust, shouting, "Gold! Gold! from the American River!" By May 15, the town's population was 200, after most fled to prospect for gold. San Francisco harbor was filled with unmanned ships, the crews having headed for the hills. Army Lt. William Sherman, surveyor of the soon-bustling streets of Old Sacramento, and later Civil War occupier of Atlanta, wrote: "Everybody was talking of 'Gold! gold!!' until it assumed the character of a fever. Some of our soldiers began to desert."

Go West, Young Man

Outside the immediate area, word spread slowly. But in December 1848, President James K. Polk announced to Congress news of the find. A vast number of Americans soon decided that making $30 a day in the gold fields beat a dollar a day behind a plow. The following year, about one hundred thousand "49ers" poured into California, two thirds of them from the U.S. Roughly 30,000 Americans rushed to California by wagon across the Great Plains, others by ship around South America. Some towns back East resembled wartime settlements, with most of their men gone, the women left to fend family and field.

Others came from Mexico, Peru, Chile, Australia, Europe, and Asia. The region had a handful of Chinese in 1848; by 1852, 20,000. By 1854, 300,000 newcomers in all had arrived. By 1856, San Francisco had 50,000 residents. It was America's greatest mass migration up to that time.

California would thereafter have a cosmopolitan hue, but relations among the different groups were testy. The region imposed a $20-a-month mining fee on the Latin American arrivals, thousands of whom headed back home.

Germs and Blue Jeans

In the gold fields, arrivals worked backbreaking 14-hour days, six days a week, moving boulders, building sluices, wading in chilly streams. About one in twelve 49ers died. Cholera took the life of every seventh Sacramento resident.

Still, about half of the diggers got a decent return from their labors. In 1849, miners dug out $10 million in gold, $250 million in today's dollars. The pay dirt topped out at $80 million in 1852, then $45 million yearly through 1857, before falling off. Merchants who outfitted, provisioned, and entertained the miners did very well. One, Levi Strauss, a Bavarian immigrant, turned tent canvas into work pants, added metal rivets for support, and made a fortune with his eponymous Levi's jeans. Diggers would pay $5 for a pound of coffee, and a premium for marks of civilization like tickets to a theater show.

As often in the West, Native Americans got the short end. Their hunting grounds were trampled over, and their fishing streams spoiled by sediments from excavations. Newcomers continued the Mexican practice of using Indians as bonded laborers. Disease ravaged the tribes, whose population was decimated.

The Wild, Wild West

With the Mexican government gone and Army rule lax, gold country was the true Wild West. Miners simply adopted the local practice of "staking a claim" on land, and losing out if the land went unused. Squatters overran Sutter's orchards and range—he died bankrupt in 1880, after bootless demands for compensation.

Boom towns were thrown up with names like Rough and Ready. Residents often dwelled in shacks and tents. In August 1850, a riot of squatters shook Sacramento. Ramshackle dwellings were fire traps. In 1849–1850, San Francisco suffered four disastrous blazes.

Women in the lawless region were very few, except for dancehall "Model Artists." Gambling and heavy drinking among the males were common. Noted one 49er: "Men make and lose thousands in a night, and frequently small boys will go up and bet $5 or 10 and if they lose all, go the next day and dig more."

CALIFORNIA DREAMIN'

Still, most arrivals put down roots. California, buoyed by new ranches and orchards, and linked by railroads and steamboats, prospered. Less than two years after the find at Sutter's Mill, residents voted 12,872 to 811 to ratify a state constitution. Slavery was banned, and the state of California entered the Union in 1850.

For a place of vast resources adopting the nickname "Golden State," and the motto, "Eureka," many more booms, and some busts—from real estate to biotech—would follow.

HAMILTON AND JEFFERSON:
DIFFERING VISIONS

The two Founding Fathers—and bitter enemies—were cordial, but cool, at their elegant dinner in the nation's temporary capital of New York City on June 20, 1790.

New York's Alexander Hamilton, Treasury Secretary of the new American government, wanted to balance the nation's books. The 13 states owed a great amount of money, and Hamilton wanted his Treasury to assume these debts dating from the Revolutionary War, and so establish the creditworthiness of the country and its new government, set up the previous year.

Virginia's Thomas Jefferson, the first Secretary of State, was wary about the debt assumption, and about much else Hamilton represented.

A STUDY IN CONTRASTS

Their conflicting views reflected the men's different backgrounds. Hamilton had served in the Revolution as a colonel under then-General Washington. Both he and Washington had been dismayed at the Continental Congress's weak support of the revolutionary army. Congress had been disorganized and short of funds; the army had been chronically short of weapons and supplies.

Further, Hamilton was a successful lawyer who often represented New York's many merchants and banks, and who saw the continued growth of the North's commerce as a boon to the nation.

Hamilton was determined to build a strong government solvent enough to fund the new army and navy. Also, for fiscal purposes, he wanted a national bank, and sought to levy a national excise tax. Soon he would call for tariffs on foreign goods to protect American industry.

Jefferson, the *de facto* leader of the opposition to the Washington Administration, distrusted a strong federal government, and wanted power retained by the states and the people. Like many prominent Southerners, he was a plantation owner often in debt to, and distrustful of, Northern and foreign creditors. Philosophically, he was suspicious of a national bank, federal excises, and a large and permanent national military. Practically, he was opposed to tariffs that would hike the price of goods imported by the nation's farmers.

For the moment, the two powerful men cut a deal. Jefferson agreed that his allies, including the Speaker of the House of Representatives, Virginian James Madison, would accept the government's assumption of the country's debt. In return, Hamilton agreed to back placement of the nation's permanent capitol in the tidewater plantation country of Virginia and Maryland, in a spot later named Washington, D.C.

America as Hybrid

In the long run, Hamilton got much of what he wanted. A strong national government. A military that grew in time to the strongest in the world. A national bank that, after many permutations, would emerge in a later century as a powerful Federal Reserve. And, with considerable help from tariffs and land grants from Washington, D.C., America became the world's preeminent industrial power.

Yet Jefferson won out in other ways. America's government remained, much more than in other nations, decentralized, with states and localities retaining considerable power. The vision of a Jeffersonian democracy, in which every man had a vote, became the norm. Even America's culture—informal, rapidly changing, and egalitarian—developed more along Jefferson's freer-thinking lines, and less along Hamilton's more formal, more aristocratic notions.

In the very long run, America "cut a deal," and reached a series of compromises, between the two conflicting views of its twin influential founders.

J. Edgar Hoover and the FBI:
The G-Men

The Justice Department's Bureau of Investigation, as it was called in 1924, was under fire. In 1922, a notorious scandal, called Teapot Dome, had erupted after Secretary of the Interior Albert Fall took bribes in return for leasing out California and Wyoming oil fields. The imbroglio implicated the Bureau, whose officials had wiretapped congressional investigators looking into the scam. Attorney General Harlan Fiske Stone wanted an able, honest man put in charge of the Bureau's 440 Special Agents. He picked 29-year-old John Edgar Hoover.

TOUGH COP

Hoover had himself received notoriety, as head of the General Intelligence section, for planning the 1919–20 "Palmer Raids." These were a series of investigations and arrests of suspected left-wing radicals undertaken by President Wilson's Attorney General, A. Mitchell Palmer. The raids took place during the Red Scare following the 1917 Russian Revolution, and a spate of anarchist bombings in the U.S., including one at the home of Attorney General Palmer. Under Hoover and Palmer's direction, 3,000 people across the country were rounded up, often without search warrants. About 600 foreigners, including radical leader Emma Goldman, were deported.

Born in Washington, D.C., on January 1, 1895, Hoover was the son of a federal-officer father and a stern, Presbyterian mother, the granddaughter of a Swiss Consul General. In high school he headed the military drill team and taught Sunday school. As a clerk at the Library of Congress, he became an expert at indexing and compiling records. After graduating from George Washington University's night law school, he joined the Justice Department in 1917. A tireless focus on detail soon made him an assistant to the Attorney General.

Hoover accepted the job heading the Bureau of Investigation, in exchange for complete control over appointments and freedom from political interference. He soon transformed the place into a U.S. version of Scotland Yard, setting up a central repository of fingerprints in 1925 that would in time house more than 90 million prints. In 1932, Hoover established a crime lab that became state-of-the-art in criminal forensics. In 1935 he founded a National Police Academy that would train generations of local and state law officers. That same year, he was made director of the expanded, renamed Federal Bureau of Investigation, the FBI.

The 1930s witnessed a nationwide skein of kidnappings, and a crime wave of highly publicized robberies and bank heists by criminals, like Machine Gun Kelly and the John Dillinger gang, who brandished heavy ordnance and employed souped-up getaway cars. Hoover's FBI cracked down. Kidnappings plummeted, and the front-page larcenists were killed or put behind bars.

Selective Investigations

The FBI chief also put together files on thousands of Americans, including suspected radicals and famous public figures. Sometimes this was done at the request of political leaders. In 1940, President Franklin Roosevelt had Hoover assemble dossiers on persons who criticized his support for the prewar American military buildup. Other, later presidents, like Harry Truman, essentially ignored Hoover's eager file gathering, while still others, including presidents John Kennedy and Richard Nixon, feared dismissing Hoover, given the huge amount of sensitive information he'd compiled.

During the 1940s, Hoover's agency busted up Nazi spy rings. In 1942, it swiftly rounded up a clique of German agents set ashore by U-boats on Long Island and Florida to commit acts of sabotage. After the war, during another red scare, Hoover targeted spies the Soviet KGB had planted in high-level government agencies.

One organization that little felt the wrath of the Director was the Mafia, whose activities Hoover usually dismissed as petty vice. It wasn't until after Hoover's death in 1972 that the FBI took on and dismantled most of America's organized crime families.

Perhaps Hoover's most controversial case was his 1960s wiretapping and harassment of civil rights leader Dr. Martin Luther King, Jr. Hoover played tapes of King's extramarital dalliances to reporters. Yet Hoover's men also quickly found, in 1965, the killers of civil rights worker Viola Liuzzo, and undermined the Ku Klux Klan by flooding it with undercover FBI plants.

Most Wanted

The most powerful law officer in U.S. history, Hoover evinced a talent for publicity that highlighted the popular side of his far-flung operations. He created a "Ten Most Wanted List" which for decades was tacked onto the walls of every post office. He wrote a best-selling, anti-Communist book, *Masters of Deceit*. He advised the producers of a popular television series, "The FBI." And for years he carefully dribbled inside information to the country's most popular newspaper columnist, Walter Winchell. Mostly under wraps was his 40-year-plus-long association—featuring almost-daily lunches and dinners—with Clyde Tolson, the Bureau's associate director. Some claimed the G-men were lovers, while confidantes described their relationship as fraternal.

When the Director passed on, after 55 years at the Justice Department, it was inevitable the Bureau's vast, if sterile-looking, new headquarters in downtown Washington would be named The J. Edgar Hoover Building. To stem too much accumulation of power, Hoover's successors were term-limited to ten years.

From forensic scrutiny of terrorist bombings abroad to take-downs of street gangs at home, Hoover's godchild, the FBI, has remained the major player in national law enforcement.

The Interstate Highway System:
Ribbons of Roads

The young military officer, and his caravan of 81 vehicles, was stuck near Emmitsburg, Maryland, in 1919. The Army had sponsored the journey to find out how long a convoy of military trucks would take to travel from coast to coast. Drivers found the roads along the Lincoln Highway, America's first cross-country thoroughfare, to be disconnected, meandering, poorly marked. Accidents occurred constantly from the stop-and-start driving. Nine of the 81 vehicles were abandoned. After 62 days, a frustrated Lt. Col. Dwight Eisenhower and his fellow troopers finally limped into San Francisco.

Twenty-six years later, near the Second World War's end, now-Gen. Eisenhower was struck by the speed with which his mechanized soldiers rolled across hostile Germany via its *autobahn* super-highways, ironically constructed to help *German* soldiers.

"Germany had made me see the wisdom of broader ribbons across the land," Eisenhower would write. "I made an absolute decision to see that the U.S. would benefit."

NATIONAL ROADS

Officials have debated the role of public infrastructure like roads and canals since the beginning of America. Through land grants and bonds, the federal government pushed along the building of the first transcontinental railroad in the 1860s. When Eisenhower became president in 1953, he pushed a federally backed interstate highway system. His Cold War–era rationale was the need to move troops, and civilians, in national emergencies. Such a network of roads, he said, would "meet the demands of catastrophe or defense, should an atomic war come."

Soon after Lt. Col. Eisenhower's difficult cross-country trip, Washington, D.C. had begun to study the idea of such a road network. In 1921 the army compiled a list of roads, the Pershing Map, named after First World War commanding general John "Black Jack" Pershing, that were deemed critical for defense. In 1938, President Franklin Roosevelt gave the Bureau of Public Roads, later the Department of Transportation, a hand-drawn map of eight highways. This led to a Bureau report calling for a 26,700-mile set of roads. In 1944, the Federal Highway Act mandated a "National System of Interstate Highways . . . to connect by routes, direct as practical, the principal metropolitan areas, cities, and industrial centers, to serve the National Defense."

In 1952 and 1954, some work was authorized, but with little funding. Congress balked at floating bonds or enacting tolls to pay for highway construction. Then Louisiana Sen. Hale Boggs came up with the notion of a "highway trust fund," its coffers filled through a federal gasoline tax. The dedicated fund picked up 90 percent of the states' construction costs. The states, and local highway authorities, not the federal government, did the construction work.

Some $114 billion would be spent on the system, $425 billion in 2006 dollars, after an initial cost estimate of $25 billion. Most of it was finished by the 1960s, then work on remaining portions dragged on into the 2000s. Federal highway spending grew into a large annual expense, amounting in 2010 to about $40 billion.

The 1956 Federal Highway Aid Act set the requirements for the system's roads: four lanes, each lane 12 feet wide, with broad shoulders, and well-defined exit and entrance ramps. North-south highways, like Route I-95, would be odd-numbered, and east-west highways even-numbered. "Beltways" going around cities got three digits, like I-695 passing by Baltimore.

THE LARGEST OF PUBLIC WORKS

What resulted may have been, in the words of Eisenhower's Commerce Secretary, "the greatest public works program in the history of the world." Forty-seven thousand miles of highway were built or incorporated into the network, along with 104 tunnels, and over 55,000 bridges, some small and others quite large, like the cable-stayed Sunshine Skyway Bridge strung across Florida's Tampa Bay. One of the longest roads, I-95, went almost 2,000 miles from Maine to Florida. Another, I-90, reached over 3,000 miles from Boston to Seattle. Texas alone has 3,200 interstate miles of the world's largest highway system.

The Interstate Highway System changed the country. Many rural towns not on the routes went into sharp decline, while others on or near the highways prospered. Old byways such as Route 66, a storied Chicago-to-Los Angeles byway, disappeared. Others like

Route 1—a slower, north-south, Atlantic coast route—lost traffic and businesses. Trucks took more and more freight away from the long-distance railroads, a romantic symbol of America, until growing energy costs put the railways back in the black.

Some bemoaned the highways' absence of scenic vistas, and a growing homogenization. "It is now possible to travel from coast to coast without seeing anything," stated Charles Kuralt of CBS, reporting from his regular TV feature, "On the Road." "From the Interstate," he said, "America is all steel guardrails and plastic signs, and every place looks and feels and sounds and smells like every other place."

Egged on by the highways, suburbs—sprawling since the Model T—grew greatly in the 1950s and after. Malls, attractive, or not, surrounded them, with countless drive-thru restaurants and franchise outlets. Many cities routed the interstates through their downtowns, which cut once-intertwined neighborhoods off from each other. Still, the system hastened commerce, sparking growth, and jobs, and permitted millions to see parts of the country theretofore out of reach.

Most would agree with a retired Eisenhower, when looking back at his handiwork in 1963: "More than any single action by the government since the end of the Second World War, this one would change the face of America."

WILLIAM LE BARON JENNEY:
SKYSCRAPER CREATOR

It was 1853, and P. T. Barnum's Grand Traveling World's Fair had stopped in New York. In a packed hall, inventor Elisha Otis stood on a platform 40 feet off the ground, and dramatically raised a sword to cut the rope, holding it in midair. Otis slashed the rope, the crowd gasped, and the platform fell—a foot or so—then hung suspended, caught by the emergency spring Otis had devised. Elevators for tall buildings, until then notoriously dangerous, would thenceforth be remarkably safe.

In the second half of the nineteenth century, various innovations led to the construction of the first high-rise buildings. Safety elevators from the Otis Elevator Co., strong, flexible Bessemer steel, Alexander Graham Bell's telephone, and central heat-ing—all these permitted people to work safely and efficiently in what were to be termed "skyscrapers." But the man who pulled all these inventions together was a Chicago architectural engineer, William Le Baron Jenney.

THE HIGH RISE'S APPRENTICE

A direct descendant of the Pilgrims of Plymouth, Massachusetts, Jenney was born in 1832, the son of the wealthy owner of a whaling firm. As a young man, Jenney sailed to the Philippines, where he was fascinated by natives constructing typhoon-proof buildings out of lightweight bamboo. In the 1850s he studied applied engineering in Paris, where he was classmate to Gustav Eiffel, the future builder of the Eiffel Tower. During the Civil War, Maj. Jenney was chief engineer to Gen. Tecumseh Sherman's Army of the Tennessee in Nashville.

By the 1870s, Americans were rapidly moving from farms to cities, placing a premium on downtown real estate. In Chicago, after the Great Fire of 1871, businesses were resurrecting the devastated downtown through the latest architectural ideas.

In 1884, Jenney began work on the ten-story Home Insurance Building. Previously, tall buildings required a massive base of stone to carry the weight of the construction, which limited the height. But Jenney turned his building inside out, centering the construction around a skeleton of Bessemer steel, with a thin exterior of masonry, and fireproof terra-cotta floors. Piers buried deep underground offered a strong foundation.

The city's inspectors, fearing the Home Insurance Building would collapse, held up construction several times. They needn't have worried: the steel was much stronger than stone, and one-third lighter than stone supports.

Forests of Urban Towers

While designing additional high rises, Jenney commuted to the University of Michigan to teach architecture, and trained a generation of influential architects. Among his protégés were Daniel Burnham, architect of New York's Flatiron Building, the downtown-wide Plan of Chicago, and Washington, D.C.'s spectacular Union Station.

Forests of taller buildings followed. By 1913, the Woolworth Building in Manhattan reached 793 feet, at 57 stories the world's highest. By 1974, with the 1,451-foot Sears Tower, Chicago again had the tallest building on the globe, before others in Malaysia and Dubai rose to the fore. Jenney's constructions set the pattern for them all.

As his mentee Burnham urged: "Little plans have no magic to stir men's blood. Make big plans."

HELEN KELLER AND
ANNE SULLIVAN:
TEACHING THE BLIND TO SEE

Twenty-one-year-old governess Anne Sullivan was having great trouble with her blind-and-deaf young charge. She'd arrived in the Alabama town of Tuscumbia in March 1887 to instruct the six-year-old girl, named Helen. When eighteen months old, the girl had lost her sight and hearing from "brain fever," possibly scarlet fever. Her behavior since had been difficult.

On meeting Sullivan, Helen had hit her, knocking out a tooth. Previously, she'd locked her mother in a closet, and knocked over her infant sister's crib.

Disabled Orphan, Outstanding Scholar

Sullivan's background had steeled her for difficult work. An impoverished orphan, her mother had died young from tuberculosis; her drunken father had beaten her, then abandoned the family. Trachoma had rendered Sullivan partly blind. Despite eyes often wracked with pain, she'd graduated from Boston's Perkins Institute for the Blind as class valedictorian.

The previous year, Helen's parents, distraught over their stricken, uncontrollable child, had approached Alexander Graham Bell, the inventor of the telephone, and an advocate for the deaf. Bell referred them to the Perkins Institute, whose director recommended his star student, Sullivan, to teach the girl. Sullivan traveled to Tuscumbia, and moved in with Helen, in a cottage outside the parents' house.

The instructor tried getting through to the girl by having her grasp common objects, like a doll, in one hand, while "finger spelling" the letters of the object in the girl's palm.

One day, outside the cottage, she poured cold water from a pump onto Helen's hand, while fingering the word, "W-A-T-E-R."

Unleashing a Love of Learning

In that instant, Helen Keller understood. "Once I knew only darkness and stillness," she later wrote. "But a little word from the fingers of another fell into my hand that clutched at emptiness and my heart leaped to the rapture of living."

Within an hour, Keller had mastered 30 more words. Within a month, she'd changed from an ungovernable child to one with steely discipline and a zealous desire to learn.

Sullivan took Keller to Perkins for special instruction. Her progress was amazing. In 1900 Keller enrolled at Radcliffe College, Harvard's sister school for women. Through the influence of author

Mark Twain, Standard Oil magnate Henry Huttleston Rogers paid for the schooling.

During college lectures, Sullivan would sit next to Keller, and rapidly finger-spell the professor's words into Keller's hand. After four years, Keller became the first deaf and blind person to gain a bachelor's degree.

While at Radcliffe, Keller—with the help of Sullivan and the latter's future husband, Harvard English teacher John Macy—began organizing notes about her experiences. *Ladies' Home Journal* paid her $3,000 for a series of articles. In 1903 she published *The Story of My Life,* which became a sensation, translated into 50 languages. Eleven other books would follow, written on Braille typewriters.

The All-Seeing Mind

Keller wrote poet John Greenleaf Whittier: "I cannot see the lovely things with my eyes, but my mind can see them all." She also learned to "hear"—by placing her fingers on the lips and voice box of the person speaking to her. In a similar way, Keller taught herself to talk.

Now the most famous disabled person in the world, Keller became an advocate for causes like women's suffrage and non-discrimination. She campaigned ceaselessly to raise funds for the American Foundation for the Blind. Sullivan, meanwhile, after a long illness, died in 1936.

From 1948 to 1957, the State Department sponsored Keller as a goodwill ambassador on trips to over 30 countries. In Italy, she made a "tactile tour" of Donatello statues. "Blindness," she noted, "has no limiting effect upon mental vision. My intellectual horizon is infinitely wide."

In 1962, the film *The Miracle Worker* won Oscars for actresses Anne Bancroft and Patty Duke, for their portrayals of Sullivan and

Keller. In 1964, Keller was awarded the Presidential Medal of Freedom. She died in 1968 at age 87.

Before Keller and Sullivan, many persons who were blind, deaf, and dumb had been consigned to prisons and lunatic asylums. After them, those with handicaps had a far better chance at a life as full as or sometimes even fuller than those lived by people free of such afflictions.

MARTIN LUTHER KING, JR.
AND THE "I HAVE A DREAM" SPEECH

"Five score years ago, a great American, in whose symbolic shadow we stand today, signed the Emancipation Proclamation," intoned the 34-year-old preacher, standing before the Lincoln Memorial. "But one hundred years later, the Negro still is not free."

The Baptist minister and civil rights leader gazed out on the throng of one quarter million, the largest the capital had ever seen.

"The life of the Negro is still sadly crippled by the manacles of segregation, and the chains of discrimination."

On a sweltering August 20, 1963, the Rev. Dr. Martin Luther King, Jr., was at the front of a massive March on Washington, a culmination of a decades-long effort to try to end official segregation in America.

The son of a preacher, and his father the son of a preacher before that, of Atlanta's Ebenezer Baptist Church, King had entered the center of the struggle in 1955. In Birmingham, Alabama, a 42-year-old black woman, Rosa Parks, had refused to sit in the "back of the bus" to which African Americans were then consigned. King, despite being arrested, despite his home being bombed, had led a year-long boycott that ended racial separation on the city's buses.

LIVING UP TO THE NATION'S IDEALS

In his Washington speech, King, urged on by friend and gospel singer Mahalia Jackson, began a stirring conclusion. As he looked out to his right, he could see, beyond the National Mall, the Jefferson Memorial.

"I have a dream, that one day this nation will rise up and live out the true meaning of its creed: 'We hold these truths to be self-evident, that all men are created equal.'"

Just that spring, King had again been in the thick of the fight, again in Birmingham. He and his organization, the Southern Christian Leadership Conference, organized boycotts of and sit-ins at businesses that refused to serve or hire blacks. In response, a city official, Theophilus "Bull" Connor, had turned police dogs and high-pressure water hoses on the demonstrators.

In Washington, King continued, to the crowd's applause, "I have a dream that one day on the red hills of Georgia, the sons of former slaves and the sons of former slave owners will be able to sit down together at the table of brotherhood!"

In Birmingham, King, along with colleague Ralph Abernathy, had deliberately employed a strategy of "non-violent confrontation," borrowed from India's independence leader Mahatma Gandhi. The city—its jails swollen with protestors, including children, its image sullied by negative, nationwide publicity—dismissed Connor, and loosened its "Jim Crow" practices of segregation.

The Crucible of His Character

At the capital, the civil rights advocate went on: "I have a dream that my four little children will one day live in a nation where they will not be judged by the color of their skin but by the content of their character."

Other organizations, such as the Congress of Racial Equality (CORE) and the Student Nonviolent Coordinating Committee (SNCC), had also filled the vast movement. Continuing protests, in St. Augustine, Florida, and other segregated cities, helped push through passage of the landmark federal Civil Rights Act of 1964. It outlawed segregation at work, in public schools, and in public accommodations like restaurants and train stations. That same year, King became the youngest person to receive the Nobel Peace Prize.

After several more years of demonstrations, arrests, FBI surveillance, and death threats, King's life ended in tragedy. On April 4, 1968, he was assassinated in Memphis, Tennessee. Fugitive convict James Earl Ray was convicted of murder.

Yet for millions, the final words of King's March on Washington speech proved prophetic:

"We will be able to speed up that day when All of God's children, black men and white men, Jews and Gentiles, Protestants and Catholics, will be able to join hands and sing in the words of the old Negro spiritual:

'Free at last! Free at last! Thank God Almighty, we are free at last!'"

LEWIS AND CLARK:
EXPEDITION FOR THE AGES

It was a rough slog for the 33 elite frontier soldiers, trekking across 2,575 miles of Missouri River wilderness. Sometimes the men had to haul their 55-foot keelboat and two pirogues, or riverboats, loaded with gear, across shallows or into strong currents. Clouds of mosquitoes swarmed; charging buffalo, hungry wolves, and eight-foot grizzly bears were constant threats.

Starting from a camp near St. Louis on May 14, 1804, they passed the future sites of Kansas City, Missouri; Omaha, Nebraska; and Sioux City, Iowa. Ten or 15 miles a day, they rowed, sailed, or walked past assorted Native American tribes—squaring off in a near firefight with the Teton Sioux. Their mission: to become the first U.S. land expedition to explore all the way to the Pacific.

PLOTTING AN EPIC JOURNEY

The spur to this unique journey was the Louisiana Purchase, concluded the year before. The U.S. had acquired from France an 820,000-square-mile expanse reaching from Louisiana to Montana. But almost nothing was known about the territory. Its natural resources were a mystery, its animal life the subject of rumors about mastodons and unicorns. The region was peopled by potentially hostile Native American tribes and bounded by the unfriendly empires of Britain and Spain. A reconnaissance was in order.

President Thomas Jefferson had been planning such a mission even before his Louisiana Purchase gave it new impetus. To lead it, he brought in two formidable men. One was lanky, 30-year-old Meriwether Lewis, a captain with the U.S. Frontier Army, and skilled at observing and writing on frontier flora and fauna. A protégé of Jefferson's from his youth, he was serving as the president's personal secretary. Lewis, Jefferson wrote, "is habituated to the woods & familiar with Indian manners and character."

To jointly lead the adventure, Lewis thought of William Clark, a veteran of the Army and the Kentucky Militia, and his former commander. Six-foot-tall like Lewis, the muscular Clark was the younger brother of George Rogers Clark, a frontier general of the Revolutionary War. William Clark, in 15 years of service, had "learned to build forts, draw maps, lead pack trains through enemy country, and fight the Indians on their ground," a historian notes. When Lewis asked him to join up, Clark, a poor speller, warmly wrote back: "My friend I assure you no man lives with whome I would perfur to undertake Such a Trip &C as your self."

Lewis and Clark prepared carefully for their journey. Lewis traveled to Philadelphia, to learn from experts about mapmaking and navigating at night by observing the stars. He also drew on Jefferson's personal library at Monticello, which had the world's largest collection of books on the American West. With a $2,500 appropriation from Congress—in the end, a total of almost $39,000 would be spent—the two captains requisitioned a mountain of equipment.

Their haul included: 15 .54-caliber prototype rifles, a fort's worth of gunpowder, and 500 rifle flints; 10 1/2 pounds of fishing lines and hooks, and 30 steel pieces for making fire; 1,100 doses of emetic to help digestion, and 3,500 doses of "disphoretic" to induce sweating during sickness; 193 pounds of boiled-down soup; and 12 pounds of soap. They also took along, as gifts for the Indians, some 288 knives, 4,600 sewing needles, and 130 rolls of tobacco.

Each man in the expedition was handpicked, and adept at specific skills like hunting and woodworking. Discipline was stern: Even before the expedition started out, several men were confined to quarters for visiting a grog store. During the trip's early stages, privates John Newman and Moses Reed were court-martialed for mutiny and desertion. One man received 100 lashes, and both were sent back downriver. Meanwhile, Lewis survived a scare after mistakenly poisoning himself by taste-testing bits of mineral ore. He recovered after downing salts to purge his stomach.

A ROUND-TRIP CONTINENTAL SLOG

At the upper end of the Missouri, near friendly Mandan Indian villages, and close to modern Bismarck, North Dakota, the expedition made winter camp. The members were visited by a French trader, Toussaint Charbonneau, and his pregnant, 16-year-old Shoshone Indian consort, Sacagawea. The couple was recruited to serve as interpreters and to help procure horses. The expedition soon had another member, Sacagawea's newborn son, Jean-Baptiste. Clark nicknamed the precocious boy "Pompy," due to his "little dancing boy" antics.

When winter broke, the co-leaders led the expedition west. In May, 1805, after the boat Sacagawea was in almost overturned, the Indian woman calmly saved vital supplies and documents from destruction. In August, Lewis, while scouting ahead across the Continental Divide, encountered a band of Shoshones. Their chief, he learned, was Sacagawea's brother. After an affecting reunion of sister and chief, the latter approved the sale of horses to the expedition. The presence of an Indian woman and her young son, meanwhile, helped to ward off Indian attacks.

In September, the expedition undertook an 11-day, 140-mile passage through the snow-laden Bitterroot Mountains. The journeyers found little game, and had to eat three of their colts. Fortunately, on the western slope a friendly tribe of Nez Percé Indians offered the soldiers dried fish, took in their horses, and helped them fashion dugout canoes.

Then the expedition traveled 640 miles via the Clearwater, Snake, and Columbia rivers, all the while taking careful readings of each river's extent and navigability. They reached the Pacific on November 24, 1805. Clark noted in his journal: "Ocean in view! O! The Joy!" The members built, and wintered at, Fort Clatsop, close to current-day Astoria, Oregon. The site for the quarters was chosen by a vote of all, including Sacagawea and York, Clark's black manservant slave, whom Clark later freed.

In March, 1806, after a miserably wet winter, the expedition began to retrace its steps. In early summer, after trekking back over the Continental Divide, the party split up to explore more lands. Clark took a southerly route with the main party including Sacagawea, who remembered some key trails from her youth. One night, Crowe Indians slipped off with half of the party's horses. Meantime, Lewis and three men headed north, where Blackfeet Indians tried to steal their weapons. In the ensuing fight, two Indians were killed. To put distance between his group and the Blackfeet, Lewis covered 100 miles in 24 hours.

Clark and Lewis met up again where the Yellowstone River joins the Missouri. There Pierre Cruzatte, a member of the group with terrible eyesight, mistakenly thinking he'd spotted an elk, shot and injured Lewis in the thigh. Undaunted, Lewis and Clark headed back down the Missouri. They bid farewell to "Pompy," Charbonneau, and Sacagawea at one of her native villages.

On September 23, 1806, after covering more than 8,000 miles, the expedition reached St. Louis. Feared for dead, they were hailed as heroes. Remarkably, after 27 months of the hardest traveling imaginable, only one member, Sergeant Charles Floyd, had died—from a burst appendix.

Effects of a Tour Majeure

The Lewis and Clark expedition exploded the notion that there was a "Northwest Passage" of easily navigable waterways through the Rockies. The expedition also unearthed a wealth of discoveries about the region. The two leaders made the first detailed maps of the area, and periodically sent back scores of mineral and plant samples, as well as live, caged animals. The many expeditions that followed made use of their findings. Most important, Lewis and Clark signaled the determination of the U.S. to explore and populate its new Louisiana Territories. The westward movement of the pioneers followed.

The subsequent lives of Lewis and Clark took wildly divergent paths. Rewarded with 1,600 acres and a bonus of $1,228, Lewis was appointed territorial governor of Upper Louisiana. Yet he proved an ineffective administrator, and drank heavily and fell into deep depressions. In 1809, he took his own life.

Captain Clark was appointed by Jefferson as a brigadier general and superintendent of Indian affairs for the Territory of Upper Louisiana. In 1813 President James Madison made him Governor of the Missouri Territory, a role he ably handled. He arranged for the publication of his and Lewis's journals, affording historians a treasure trove. Clark married, and named a son Meriwether Lewis Clark. He also adopted, after Sacagawea's death, her son Pompy and daughter Lisette. The former, taking after his mother and adoptive father, became a skilled interpreter and scout in the Western mountains.

Lincoln's Addresses:
Words from a Peerless Statesman

Seven Southern states had already seceded from the Union. The president-elect had traveled secretly at night to Washington, D.C., to thwart a rumored assassination plot, and the real chance of anti-Union rioters meeting him in Baltimore. On March 4, 1861, along Pennsylvania Avenue, a cordon of armed Federal troops lined his inaugural parade route.

As the new President took his oath of office, above him rose, with heavy symbolism, the scaffolded dome of the Capitol, its ongoing reconstruction but partway complete.

In addition to serving as Chief Executive during the Civil War, Abraham Lincoln was perhaps the finest orator and writer of all American presidents. His two inaugural addresses, and his speech inaugurating a national cemetery at the Gettysburg battlefield, are among the nation's most famed and poetic documents. Lincoln displayed an ability to transmute into the American English of the 1860s his command of the King James Bible, Shakespeare, and classical literature, as well as momentous issues of the day.

THE FIRST INAUGURAL SPEECH

Hoping to head off war while at the same time wishing to signal strength, Lincoln chose a balanced approach. While he spoke before a large and expectant crowd, his real audience was the region in secession. The new President pledged not to alter slavery where it already existed, while insisting the Union was eternal and unbreakable. "No government proper," he asserted, "ever had a provision in its organic law for its own termination."

He ended with a stirring call for unity among divided countrymen:

"I am loath to close. We are not enemies, but friends . . . Though passion may have strained it must not break our bonds of affection.

"The mystic chords of memory, stretching from every battlefield and patriot grave to every living heart and hearthstone all over this broad land, will yet swell the chorus of the Union, when again touched, as surely they will be, by the better angels of our nature."

The choice of terms was fortuitous. Lincoln had originally planned to end his speech with the words, "Shall it be peace or sword?" However, his adviser and future Secretary of State, William Seward, convinced him to close with a more compromising call.

THE GETTYSBURG SPEECH

On November 19, 1863, Lincoln journeyed to Gettysburg, Pennsylvania to speak at the opening of a Soldiers' National Cemetery, honoring the troops who'd died at the battle there the previous July. About 46,000 men had been killed or wounded on both sides.

Before the assembled throng of 15,000, Lincoln had a difficult act to follow. The prior speaker was Edward Everett of Massachusetts, a former Secretary of State, U.S. Senator, and head of Harvard University—and a noted orator. Everett gave an impressive speech lasting two hours.

The President spoke for a bit more than two minutes, uttering 272 words.

He made two main points. One was to honor the fallen:

"We have come to dedicate a portion of that field, as a final resting place for those who here gave their lives that that nation might live . . . But, in a larger sense, we cannot dedicate—we cannot consecrate—we cannot hallow—this ground. The brave men, living and dead, who struggled here, have consecrated it, far above our poor power to add or detract. The world will little note, nor long remember what we say here, but it can never forget what they did here."

The other theme was to cast the long and bloody war as a crusade for freedom and democracy:

"Four score and seven years ago our fathers brought forth on this continent, a new nation, conceived in Liberty, and dedicated to the proposition that all men are created equal. Now we are engaged in a great civil war, testing whether that nation, or any nation so conceived and so dedicated, can long endure . . . that from these honored dead we take increased devotion to that cause for which they gave the last full measure of devotion . . . that this nation, under God, shall have a new birth of freedom—and that government of the people, by the people, for the people, shall not perish from the earth."

In this grand paragraph's opening phrase, Lincoln echoed the Psalms' description of a man's life span as "threescore years and ten; and if by reason of strength they be fourscore years." He then deliberately quoted the Declaration of Independence's phrase of "all men are created equal." Next, his phrase "the last full measure of devotion" entered the American lexicon. Then the President uttered perhaps his most famous phrase: "government of the people, by the people, for the people."

The following day, Everett wrote Lincoln: "I should be glad if I could flatter myself that I came as near to the central idea of the occasion, in two hours, as you did in two minutes." Lincoln proved less a judge of rhetoric than Everett, telling an official about his own talk: "That speech won't scour. It is a flat failure."

THE SECOND INAUGURAL SPEECH

The President's second inaugural address took place on a rain-drenched March 4, 1865. The war, and Lincoln's life, were approaching the end. John Wilkes Booth, who would murder the President in April, watched Lincoln speak from just yards away.

Drawing heavily from the Old and New Testaments, the President made remarkable comments on how the two hostile sides had not anticipated the conflict's sweeping consequences:

"Neither party expected for the war the magnitude or the duration which it has already attained . . . Each looked for an easier triumph, and a result less fundamental and astounding.

"Both read the same Bible and pray to the same God, and each invokes His aid against the other . . . The prayers of both could not be answered. That of neither has been answered fully. The Almighty has His own purposes."

INSIDE LINCOLN'S MIND

In a private, written "meditation" discovered after his death, Lincoln had shed light on his thinking: "In great contests each party claims to act in accordance with the will of God. Both may be, and one must be wrong. God cannot be for, and against the same thing at the same time. In the present civil war it is quite possible that God's purpose is somewhat different from the purpose of either party . . . "

Lincoln also presented the great costs of the war as a kind of atonement for slavery:

"Fondly do we hope, fervently do we pray, that this mighty scourge of war may speedily pass away. Yet, if God wills that it continue until all the wealth piled by the bondsman's two hundred and fifty years of unrequited toil shall be sunk, and until every drop of blood drawn with the lash shall be paid by another drawn with the sword, as was said three thousand years ago, so still it must be said 'the judgments of the Lord are true and righteous altogether.'"

As at his first inaugural, Lincoln ended on a rising note of reconciliation:

"With malice toward none, with charity for all, with firmness in the right as God gives us to see the right, let us strive on to finish the work we are in, to bind up the nation's wounds, to care for him who shall have borne the battle and for his widow and his orphan, to do all which may achieve and cherish a just and lasting peace among ourselves and with all nations."

Portions of Lincoln's speeches are etched on the walls of the Lincoln Memorial, on the other end of the National Mall from the Capitol where he delivered several of the most famous.

CHARLES LINDBERGH:
PIONEER OF LONG-DISTANCE FLIGHT

The 25-year-old aviator piloted his single-engine biplane eastward ten feet above the Atlantic's waves. He'd been up for over 55 hours, before and during the 3,300-mile flight, and had to prop open his eyelids with his fingers. The previous night he'd steered by the stars, now he reckoned by compass. He couldn't see the wave caps directly ahead, as the extra-large fuel tank blocked his view, so he glanced around the obstacle with a makeshift periscope. At times, storm clouds appeared, and he'd sweep his plane above the rain up to 10,000 feet.

"I live only in the moment in this strange, unmortal space," he reflected, "crowded with beauty, pierced with danger."

PRELUDES AND PREPARATIONS

The run-up to the May 1927 flight was challenging too. Days before, he'd left San Diego for Long Island, New York, via St. Louis. In so doing, navigating by a Rand-McNally railroad map, he'd broken the cross-continental speed record.

In New York, rain grounded him for eight days. Finally, the forecast improved, but nervousness and the all-night poker games of the reporters nearby cheated him of sleep. At 7:52 a.m. he took off, his gasoline-heavy Wright-Bellanca craft barely clearing the tree line. He was spotted above Nova Scotia, then observers lost sight of him.

He was ready for the challenge. For years, he'd "barnstormed" the United States with other early-aviation pilots, wowing the crowds with figure eights and spiraling tailspins, or propping himself on the wings of a speeding plane. He'd flown the first air-mail route from St. Louis to Chicago, landing at night by flashlight, crashing twice, to walk away and arrange the delivery of salvaged mail by truck. Thirty-one of the first 40 airmail pilots died on the job.

Now, others were also trying to fly across the Atlantic, fatally. In the week before his own flight, two French pilots had been lost in the ocean flying westward from France.

THE MOST RECOGNIZED MAN IN THE WORLD

At length, Charles Augustus Lindbergh looked down, and spotted the Irish coast. "It is like spring after a Northern winter," he recalled. "I know how the dead would feel to live again." He flew down the Seine to Paris, the first man to fly solo across the Atlantic in a heavier-than-air craft. He also became the most famous man on the planet. A mob of 150,000 Frenchmen stormed his craft, *The Spirit of St. Louis*. "I found myself on top of the crowd," Lindbergh remembered, "in the center of an ocean of heads."

Lindbergh was summoned to Washington, D.C. aboard the USS *Memphis.* President Calvin Coolidge awarded him the country's first Distinguished Flying Cross, and Congress the Medal of Honor. He was deluged with 3.5 million letters; 4 million spectators saw his Broadway ticker-tape parade. *Time* magazine made him its first Man of the Year; he is still its youngest.

The fledgling U.S. aviation industry went into overdrive. Promoting aeronautics in his *The Spirit of St. Louis,* Lindbergh flew to all 48 states; 30 million people saw him. The number of U.S. airline passengers soared in four years from under 6,000 to over 173,000. Flight pioneer Elinor Smith Sullivan recalled: "People seemed to think we [flyers] were from outer space. But after Lindbergh, we could do no wrong."

A SERIES OF CURTAIN CALLS

On a goodwill trip to Mexico, Lindbergh fell for the U.S. ambassador's daughter, Anne Spencer Morrow. They married and were to have six children. Mrs. Lindbergh, the first woman to obtain a glider pilot's license, became her husband's navigator. Together they charted many now-well-traveled air routes, such as West Africa to Brazil and the Great Circle-Polar route. They also endured the kidnapping and murder of their firstborn son, Charles, Jr., followed by the execution of the murderer after the "trial of the century."

Later, with great controversy, Lindbergh evinced sympathy for Nazi Germany, then became a war hero pilot in the Second World War's fight against fascism. He followed with a Pulitzer Prize-winning autobiography brought to the screen by American icon Jimmy Stewart. He also fathered, it was learned after his death, numerous children with multiple German mistresses. This complex, contradictory man even coinvented the first heart pump, and became an advocate of protecting the blue whale as well as native African and Filipino tribes.

Soon after his epic flight, Lindbergh secured funding from the Guggenheim family to support the farseeing rocket research of scientist Robert Goddard. In July 1969, Goddard's work bore its greatest fruit, when *Apollo 11* astronauts made the first Moon landing. Fittingly, an elderly Lindbergh watched the liftoff from Cape Kennedy.

THE LOUISIANA PURCHASE:
THE GREATEST REAL ESTATE DEAL

The most powerful man on Earth, French Emperor Napoleon Bonaparte, and the president of a small, fledgling power, Thomas Jefferson, were in a quandary over related pieces of real estate. The greatest land deal in history resulted.

In 1802, Americans were shaken by news that Spain would transfer ownership of its vast Louisiana territories, stretching for 828,000 square miles from New Orleans up to modern-day Montana, to the French. New Orleans was the port through which America's Western states shipped much of their commerce. Napoleon was seeking to re-establish French sway in North America and the nearby Caribbean. If the ambitious French leader denied New Orleans to U.S. ships, he could strangle America's economy, and perhaps invade its turf.

Diplomatic Intrigues

A worried President Jefferson gave his minister to France, Robert Livingston, instructions to try to buy New Orleans, and if possible the Florida territories to the east, for $2 million. When the Spanish blocked American cargo from New Orleans, Jefferson upped the ante to $10 million. He also sent his protégé, future president James Monroe, to Paris to aid Livingston. The president wrote Monroe: "All eyes, all hopes, are now fixed on you, for on the event of this mission depends the future destinies of this republic."

Napoleon, meanwhile, had his own concerns. He was ever at war in Europe, and badly short of funds. In the Western Hemisphere, he had tried to re-conquer the rich island of Santo Domingo—modern-day Haiti and the Dominican Republic. However, yellow fever and the slave revolt of François-Dominique Toussaint L'Ouverture had worn down the 40,000-man French occupying force.

Meantime, a friend of Jefferson's, French nobleman Pierre Samuel du Pont de Nemours—whose progeny would found the U.S. chemical firm DuPont—was working behind the scenes. Du Pont de Nemours came up with a novel idea, adopted by Napoleon's finance minister, François Barbé-Marbois. Both men realized that, without securing Santo Domingo, the port city of New Orleans and adjacent territories would be far less valuable to France. The finance minister urged Napoleon to cut his losses.

On April 12, 1802, when Monroe arrived in Paris, Livingston greeted him with startling news. The day before, the powerful French foreign minister, Charles Maurice de Talleyrand, had offered the U.S. all the Louisiana territories, for $15 million. The American envoys knew it would take weeks, via slow-moving sailing ships, to get approval from home. So they accepted Napoleon's offer on their own authority.

Domestic Politicking

When word reached America, the nation was split. Jefferson's foes in the opposition Federalist party saw the purchase as a power grab to benefit his allies in the West and South. Massachusetts senator Timothy Pickering pushed for Federalist New England to secede from the U.S., and offered to make Vice President Aaron Burr president of the resulting new nation. Jefferson himself doubted the Constitution gave him authority to purchase new lands.

Faced with such a land bargain, however, the "Red Fox" concluded: "It is the case of a guardian, investing the money of his ward in purchasing an important adjacent territory; and saying to him when of age, I did this for your good." A divided House of Representatives approved the deal by a vote of 59–57.

The Louisiana Purchase was paid for with $3 million of U.S. gold, the rest in American bonds. The bonds were discounted by the cash-starved French; in the end the transaction totaled only $8.8 million.

Expansion Then, and Thereafter

In November 1803, the U.S. raised its flag over New Orleans. The following March, the U.S. formally took control of the territories, at the de facto territorial capital of St. Louis. An official on hand was Meriwether Lewis, soon to help lead, with William Clark, an expedition through the newly acquired lands.

The Louisiana Purchase brought the United States, along with New Orleans, all of present-day Arkansas, Iowa, Kansas, Nebraska, and Oklahoma—as well as portions of Colorado, Louisiana, Montana, Minnesota, New Mexico, North Dakota, South Dakota, and Wyoming.

The price, in today's dollars, was about $200 million—under 4 cents an acre. Revolutionary War hero Gen. Horatio Gates informed Jefferson: "Let the Land rejoice, for you have bought Louisiana for a Song." The Purchase also led, four decades later, to war with Mexico over disputed lands southwest of Louisiana, and to the acquisition of the American Southwest. It also brought on the acquisition of the Pacific Northwestern states of Oregon and Washington. Napoleon commented: "This accession of territory affirms forever the power of the United States."

THE MANHATTAN PROJECT:
BUILDING A BIGGER BOMB

The smartest men in the world were about to test-fire a weapon that could end civilization—and they were acting silly. Enrico Fermi, the Nobel Prize–winning Italian physicist, jokingly bet on "whether the bomb would ignite the atmosphere." A nervous Robert Oppenheimer, the program's lead scientist, wagered a colleague, an expert in plutonium, ten dollars that the bomb would fizzle.

On July 16, 1945, the esteemed group of scientists, engineers, and government officials were gathered on a remote bombing range south of the town of Los Alamos, New Mexico—locally called *La Jornada del Muerto,* the Journey of Death. The test was code-named, with little pretension, Trinity.

At 5:30 a.m., their uranium device went off—with the force of 21,000 tons of TNT. For the first time in history, a giant mushroom-shaped cloud rose up from a nuclear blast. Oppenheimer's colleague, five miles from the test site, was knocked off his feet. He cuffed his boss, exclaiming, "Oppie, you owe me ten dollars!"

NUCLEAR AMBITIONS

More soberly, Oppenheimer reflected on the consequences of the massive program, code-named the Manhattan Project—Washington's crash effort to construct an atomic weapon. He recalled an ancient Hindu text: "Now I am become Death, the destroyer of worlds." More practically, the project's military chief, Gen. Leslie Groves, stated the Second World War was now all but over—"after we drop two bombs on Japan."

The genesis of the atomic bomb had been the growing power in the late 1930s of Japan's ally, Nazi Germany, and the fear among European scientists opposed to Adolph Hitler that the German dictator would be the first to build a nuclear bomb.

In December 1938, scientists in Berlin had managed to "split the atom," dividing the nuclei of uranium atoms, and generating energy as a result. In theory, a chain reaction of such nuclear "fission" could generate enough energy for a great explosion. The following August, Albert Einstein—the renowned German-Jewish physicist who'd fled Hitler to teach at Princeton University—composed a letter to President Franklin Roosevelt. Citing the Nazi breakthrough, Einstein warned the president that "extremely powerful bombs of a new type may thus be constructed."

After Japan's December 1941 attack on Pearl Harbor, and Germany's declaration of war on the U.S., the War Department mounted a gigantic effort to build such a bomb.

Constructing a City Buster

Leading the effort was Gen. Groves, an organizational genius who forced through the construction of the Pentagon, the world's largest office building, in just 16 months. For the Manhattan Project, the no-nonsense Groves managed a workforce of 125,000, and the construction and operation of 30 far-flung sites, including four major facilities.

These latter sites included a plant in Hanford, Washington, to mass-produce plutonium. A 60,000-acre complex in Oak Ridge, Tennessee, produced the other main component for building bombs—uranium. At the University of Chicago, scientists constructed an "atomic pile" of uranium and graphite to make small amounts of plutonium for the Hanford plant. At the University, Fermi worked with U.S. chemist Glenn Seaborg, the discoverer of ten elements, including plutonium, to orchestrate the first atomic chain reaction. The reaction took place in the first nuclear reactor ever built; it was conducted for secrecy under the school's Stagg Field football stadium.

The fourth major installation was Los Alamos, located on the site of a former ranching school. It hosted the research center where the leading scientists brainstormed. And technicians there assembled components from the other sites into complete bombs.

The cost of the program, in 2010 dollars, was $29 billion. As a comparison, the cost of building all the U.S. tanks in the war was $90 billion. Seventy million pounds of silver were used in a single, and unsuccessful, method of separating radioactive isotopes. The largest expenses were for Oak Ridge, which drew on the Tennessee Valley Authority for electrical power. Energy demands there sometimes consumed more than 15 percent of all U.S. electricity.

A HALL OF FAME ROSTER

A key decision of Groves was to pick Oppenheimer, aged 38, to direct the scientists. Oppenheimer assembled and deftly managed an unmatched collection of talent.

Along with Fermi, who'd fled fascist strongman Benito Mussolini's Italy, Oppenheimer was joined by mathematician John von Neumann, a Hungarian immigrant who was later a major force behind the first computers; Nils Bohr, a Nobel Prize–winning Danish émigré who'd discovered much of the atom's inner workings; Edward Teller, another Hungarian immigrant, the postwar father of the even more powerful hydrogen bomb; and New York–born Richard Feynman, later a leading theorist of nanotechnology. Another vital player was Ernest Lawrence, of Berkeley's Radiation Laboratory, who—through his invention of the cyclotron, or atom smasher—had helped make the U.S. the world leader in nuclear engineering.

Project security was so tight that the wartime governor of Tennessee never learned about the sprawling Oak Ridge site. Yet penetrating deep into the program was the Soviet Union's spy agency, the KGB. British physicist and Soviet agent Klaus Fuchs was posted to Los Alamos, where he passed on data about nuclear weapons design. From the site's engineering department, KGB spy David Greenglass handed top-secret information to his sister Ethel Rosenberg, later executed with her husband for espionage.

Still, after just 33 months, the Manhattan Project successfully tested the atomic bomb. Then, on August 6, 1945, Gen. Groves' prophecy about Japan began to come true, when an American B-29 dropped a uranium bomb on the city of Hiroshima, destroying 70 percent of its buildings. On August 9, a plutonium bomb was dropped on the city of Nagasaki, generating winds of 624 mph and heat of 7,000 degrees. Six days later, Japan surrendered, ending the war. Over 100,000 people were killed by the two bombs.

The program had changed military science, and the world, irrevocably.

Justice John Marshall:
Supreme Interpreter of the
Constitution

It was the political trial of the young century. In the Richmond, Virginia federal circuit court room in 1807, Aaron Burr, President Jefferson's former vice president, and killer, in a duel, of former Treasury Secretary Alexander Hamilton, was on trial for treason. Jefferson alleged Burr had conspired to detach the Western territories of the United States to form a separate country. The presiding judge—U.S. Supreme Court Chief Justice John Marshall—acquitted Burr. Marshall ruled the prosecution had failed to produce, as the Constitution stipulated in cases of treason, the testimony of at least two witnesses.

Making a Court Supreme

Throughout his 34 years as chief justice, John Marshall made the Supreme Court the final arbiter of the Constitution. What had been a weak appendage to the federal government became in time a branch of government practically coequal to Congress and the president.

Four years before the Burr trial, Marshall established the Court's "right of judicial review," whereby it could overrule the legislative or executive branches if either violated the Constitution.

The case in question was *Marbury v. Madison.* Before leaving office in 1801, President John Adams had appointed William Marbury to a federal judgeship. Upon succeeding Adams, his political rival, President Jefferson had refused to seat Marbury. Jefferson and his congressional allies also had repealed the act of Congress which created Adams' new judgeships. So Marbury sued James Madison, Jefferson's secretary of state, demanding he grant him his job.

Marshall was in a bind. An ally of Adams, whom had appointed him chief justice, Marshall had sympathy for Marbury. But Jefferson's allies threatened to impeach Marshall if he reestablished the act creating the new judgeships. Marshall cleverly ruled that, while Marbury should receive a judgeship, a congressional law allowing his Court to compel Marbury to assume a judgeship was unconstitutional.

Landmark Cases

Thus Marshall successfully asserted the power of the Court to declare acts of Congress unconstitutional and, by implication, presidential acts. He'd taken a huge stride toward making the Constitution the supreme law of the land, and the Supreme Court its ultimate interpreter.

Other big decisions followed. In 1819's *Dartmouth College v. Woodward,* his Court ruled invalid the New Hampshire legislature's attempt to make Dartmouth College, a private school, a public institution. The ruling considerably strengthened private property rights in the new nation, while asserting the right of the Court to overrule state decisions. Also that year, in *McCulloch v. Maryland,* the Marshall Court rejected Maryland's attempt to tax the federal government's Second Bank of the United States, a bank that Maryland held the Constitution had not explicitly authorized. In upholding the bank's legality, the Court ruled the Constitution grants the government implicit powers not expressly stated in its text, under its "necessary and proper" clause, to enable establishment of an effective national government.

In 1824's *Gibbons v. Ogden,* the Marshall Court, to spur competition, ruled against a monopoly over New York's steamboat business run by a group including Robert Fulton, the steamboat's inventor. The Court stated that the federal government, through Congress, had the power to regulate interstate commerce.

Marshall himself wrote 519 of his Court's 1,100 opinions. Possessing a marked ability to influence his fellow justices, he had to write only eight dissenting opinions.

JUDICIAL GIANT

Like his distant descendant, Secretary of State and Second World War Army Chief of Staff George Marshall, John Marshall had the background to be president. He never became one, while wielding, like his relation, more influence than most presidents.

Born in 1755 in a log cabin on the Virginia frontier, he was the oldest of 15 children. During the Revolution he was a lieutenant in the Minutemen militia, then an officer with Colonel Daniel Morgan's elite foot soldiers. At Valley Forge, he was General Washington's top legal officer, presiding over hundreds of court martials. After the war he wrote a five-volume biography of Washington.

Before making him chief justice, Adams entrusted Marshall with the vital role of envoy to France during the Undeclared Naval War with that country. At that time, during the XYZ Affair, French agents unsuccessfully tried to bribe Marshall and the other American diplomats.

When he was absent from Washington, D.C., Marshall resided in Richmond, Virginia, and became that burgeoning city's leading citizen, founding its fire department, insurance company, and library.

At age 27, Marshall proposed to Yorktown, Virginia–born Mary Ambler, age 16, called by Jefferson the "Fair Belinda." A nervous Ambler declined Marshall's suggestion and, after his departure, burst out crying with regret. Her cousin rode off to tell Marshall of the change of heart, with a lock of Mary's hair as a token. Marshall sent back a lock of his own hair, which was intertwined with Mary's in a locket. The two married and had ten children.

Cyrus McCormick:
Mechanized Farming Feeds a Nation

In 1830, about 85 percent of Americans lived on farms. As had been done since ancient times, farmers would laboriously cut down the yearly harvest with a wood-and-metal scythe, then with backbreaking work bundle and store the grain. A farmer could harvest just one to three acres a day.

That all started to change in 1831, when a 22-year-old from Virginia's Shenandoah Valley put together the first mechanical, horse-drawn reaper. The bulky device clattered loudly, and looked strange—"a cross between a wheelbarrow, a chariot, and a flying machine," as the *London Times* reported. Yet its gears and wheel propelled the reaper's moving parts, felling crops at a much swifter rate.

The young farmhand, Cyrus McCormick, could clear 12 acres a day with his creation.

Like Father, Like Cyrus

Cyrus' father Robert was the owner of a prosperous, 530-acre farm. For about 20 years, he'd labored unsuccessfully to build a mechanical reaper. His son had shown talent, however, inventing a lightweight cart for towing away grain, at age 15. Cyrus was determined to fulfill his father's dream. In short order, working from the family farm's blacksmith shop, he succeeded.

For years, sales of his newfangled implement were nil. Harvests had been brought in by hand since time immemorial; farmers doubted McCormick's reaper would work or be worth the money. The young mechanic spent long years improving his invention. In time he was able to gather 50 acres a day with it. By 1844, McCormick was selling 50 reapers a year. However, many firms with whom he contracted to build the machines backed out of deals or failed to make payments.

McCormick battled back by creating new methods to improve the business of selling the reapers. He offered farmers written guarantees—"15 acres a day or your money back!"—and monthly payment plans. Many farmers abandoned the harvesters when they couldn't figure out how they worked, so McCormick trained his salesmen to demonstrate the devices. Among the first traveling salesmen, they hawked the reapers all over the Midwest. McCormick hired some of his best customers as sales agents, paying them commissions. One, James Hite—who'd employed a McCormick reaper to harvest 175 acres in little more than a week—supplied his boss with a catchy sales tag: "My reaper has more than paid for itself in one harvest!"

At the same time, McCormick protected the patents for his machines by taking competitors to court, backed by the best legal talent of the day, including future Civil War Secretary of War Edwin Stanton, and Stanton's future boss—Illinois barrister Abraham Lincoln. By 1847, McCormick was selling 500 reapers annually.

A REVOLUTION ON THE FARM, AND FOR THE CITIES

Freeing himself from unreliable manufacturers, and to greatly expand production, McCormick built his own factory. He picked an ideal location: Chicago, near the Midwest's vast and increasingly cultivated prairies. City boosters, like Illinois Sen. Stephen A. Douglas and railroad magnate William Ogden, were planning railways and canals to make Chicago a transportation and manufacturing hub. Ogden became McCormick's first financial backer, investing $25,000. Established in 1848, McCormick's assembly plant had hired 120 workers within two years.

Constantly improving his reaper, McCormick won plaudits overseas, winning the Gold Medal at the 1851 World's Fair in London's Crystal Palace. He was appointed to France's Academy of Sciences, which lauded him for doing "more for agriculture than any other living man." Aided by his younger brothers—Leander McCormick supervised production, while William ran the books—sales of the reaper surpassed 4,000 in 1860. The machines allowed farmers to put vast new areas of the Midwest under the plow. Lincoln's secretary of state, William Seward, noted that the McCormick reaper moves "the line of civilization westward thirty miles each year."

McCormick's harvester, along with a plethora of other agricultural innovations, pushed the spectacular productivity of America's farmers, and the nation's rush to the cities. By 2010, one American farmer grew enough to feed 155 people, many of them overseas. And 98 percent of Americans resided in suburbs and cities.

THE BATTLE OF MIDWAY:
A MIRACLE HALFWAY ACROSS THE OCEAN

Injured navy pilot, Ensign George Gay, Jr., treaded water in the middle of the Pacific, dodging Japanese warships. Earlier that morning of June 4, 1942, Gay and his squadron of Devastator torpedo planes had attacked a fleet of Japanese aircraft carriers steaming for the strategic atoll of Midway, 1,100 miles northwest of Hawaii. Yet nimble "Zero" fighters had jumped on the lumbering, lightly armed U.S. aircraft, shooting them all down, killing 29 of the squadron's 30 men.

After a pancake landing in the ocean, Gay had scrambled out of his sinking plane. Floating in a life vest, he had a clear view of three enemy carriers: the *Akagi, Kaga,* and *Soryu.*

BOUNCING UP FROM A KNOCK-OUT PUNCH

The morning had thus far yielded more setbacks in the Second World War's Pacific theater. On December 7, 1941, Japanese carrier planes had devastated much of the U.S. fleet at Pearl Harbor. Japan soon seized control of Malaysia, the Dutch East Indies (today Indonesia), Singapore, and the Philippines, then a U.S. commonwealth.

Now Tokyo aimed to sink the remnants of the U.S. Navy, and force Washington into peace talks. Admiral Isoroku Yamamoto, architect of the Pearl Harbor assault, put together the plan of attack. Vice Admiral Chuichi Nagumo, who'd carried out the Pearl Harbor raid, commanded the fleet of four carriers, 229 aircraft, and supporting ships. It was backed up by two other arrays of battleships, light carriers, cruisers, and destroyers, as well as transport ships carrying Imperial Marines to seize Midway.

However, the U.S. Navy was waiting and ready. Months before, intelligence experts had broken the Japanese navy's code. Cryptanalysts had deciphered the names of the ships in the oncoming fleet and the date of their arrival off Midway.

U.S. Marines and airmen prepped the atoll against a seaborne invasion. And U.S. Pacific Fleet commander Admiral Chester Nimitz ordered the carriers USS *Enterprise* and *Hornet*, skippered by Admiral Ray Spruance, to lay in ambush east of Midway. They were joined, almost miraculously, by the carrier USS *Yorktown*, which the Japanese believed they had sunk months before. Severely damaged, she'd been towed to Pearl Harbor where, in just 72 hours, mechanics had patched up her superstructure and flight deck.

SACRIFICES LEADING TO SUCCESS

At 6:30 a.m. on June 4, aircraft from the Japanese carriers raided Midway, but failed to knock out its air base. Earlier, a U.S. patrol plane had spotted the Japanese fleet. In response, the Americans launched a series of piecemeal raids from their three carriers and from Midway. Yet the navy torpedo planes, Marine Corps bombers, and long-range army Air Force B-26 bombers failed to hit a single ship. Carrier-launched Zeros knocked most of them out of the sky.

Meantime, Nagumo ordered his returning pilots to prepare to again attack the Midway airfield. Soon after, however, a Japanese patrol plane spotted a U.S. carrier, and radioed word back. Nagumo, alarmed, ordered a switch to an attack on the U.S. fleet. This entailed the time-consuming labor of replacing the aircrafts' aerial bombs with anti-ship ordnance. Then Ensign Gay's torpedo planes, and two other squadrons from the *Enterprise, Hornet,* and *Yorktown* made their attacks. Although shot out of the sky, they delayed the launch of the next Japanese air wave, and stripped the carriers of the Zeros' protective cover.

Fatefully, three more squadrons of U.S. planes—Dauntless dive bombers from the *Enterprise* and *Yorktown*—then appeared overhead. One squadron was nearly out of enough fuel for a return flight, but its leader, Lieutenant Commander C. Wade McClusky, Jr., gambling he could get his planes home, had pressed on.

A Fiery Turning Point

The Japanese carriers—devoid of air cover, their decks crammed with high explosives and refueling planes—were caught flat-footed. The dive bombers swooped in, scoring direct hits.

Flight commander Mitsuo Fuchida, a squadron chief at Pearl Harbor, witnessed the attack from the *Akagi:* "As the fire spread among planes lined up wing to wing on the after flight deck, their torpedoes began to explode," he recalled. "The entire hangar area was a blazing inferno."

Ensign Gay, floating just hundreds of yards from the carriers, had a ringside seat, "cheering and hollering with every hit." Three carriers were set ablaze, and sank.

Several hours later, bombers from the remaining Japanese carrier the *Hiryu* severely damaged the *Yorktown*. A Japanese submarine later sunk the gallant ship, after its crew transferred to other vessels. American carrier planes, meantime, sank the *Hiryu*. A shocked Admiral Yamamoto ordered his fleet to retire.

Japan had lost its major maritime striking force—the very same carriers that had devastated Pearl Harbor. Over 2,000 Japanese were dead, including more than 200 experienced, irreplaceable pilots. Over 330 precious aircraft were destroyed. The U.S. lost 350 sailors and airmen.

When Ensign Gay died in 1994, his ashes were scattered over the position where his squadron's fellow pilots had sacrificed themselves in 1942, leading to the incredible victory of Midway.

SAMUEL MORSE:
ORIGINAL INSTANT MESSAGING

In April 2009, Google marked the birthday of inventor Samuel Finley Morse by displaying his name on its home page—in Morse code, which he devised while helping invent the telegraph. Google was itself a latter-day result of U.S. ingenuity in electrical and electronic applications that stretched from Ben Franklin's lightning rods to Morse's telegraph lines to today's instantaneous, Web- and satellite-centered applications.

Morse, the son of a fierce Calvinist preacher, was born in 1791 in Charlestown, Massachusetts. He was to become famous in several fields. A graduate of the elite Phillips Academy, he earned a Phi Beta Kappa at Yale, where he studied religion and mathematics, and soaked up lectures on electricity.

THE TECHNO-WIZ AS ARTIST

In his first career, he was a nationally known artist, serving as Professor of Painting and Sculpture at New York University (NYU). A focus was history; he painted portraits of former President John Adams and Revolutionary War icon Marquis de Lafayette.

Morse was also deeply interested in politics, though there he met with little success. An opponent of large-scale, legal immigration by Irish and German Catholics, Morse ran for mayor of immigrant-rich New York City, and garnered only 1,500 ballots. During an overseas stay in Rome, a Swiss Guardsman knocked Morse's hat off when he declined to doff it before the Pope.

His collegiate love of technology proved long-lasting and triumphant. Bridging the gap between science and art, Morse wrote a widely publicized commentary on the daguerreotype, an early form of photography. It stated: "By a simple and easily portable apparatus, the artist can now furnish his studio with fac-simile sketches of nature, landscapes, buildings, groups of figures . . . not, as heretofore, subjected to his imperfect, sketchy translations into crayon or Indian ink drawings, and occupying days, and even weeks, in their execution; but painted by Nature's self."

In 1832, while returning by ship from a European tour, Morse attended demonstrations of the recently invented electromagnet. (An electromagnet is a magnet that runs on electricity. The current or signal of the wire leading to the magnet can be altered to vary the magnet's strength.) Morse realized that by varying the signals, and attaching a reading device to the magnet, one could send and receive messages over long distances.

Others were thinking likewise. By the late 1830s, English professor Charles Wheatstone had built a 13-mile telegraph line for a British railroad. However, his telegraph was cumbersome: it had a bundle of 26 wires, one for each letter of the alphabet.

Morse Code and Distant Messaging

Through painstaking experiments over six years, Morse devised a telegraph—made of clock gears, wood, and printing-press parts—that sent signals over one wire. His first model generated a wavy line, rather like an EKG, on a piece of tape. The recipient, using a code book, translated the ups and downs of the line into letters and numbers. Morse then built a telegraph that inscribed on ticker paper various short dots and long dashes, representing letters and digits. It was dubbed Morse code. Later telegraphs dispensed with paper, and operators rapidly interpreted the beeping sound of signals by ear.

For his work, Morse had the support of excellent mentors, and a world-class mechanic. Leonard Gale, a Professor of Chemistry at NYU, introduced Morse to the research of Princeton's Joseph Henry. Back in 1831, Henry had theorized about telegraphs, and Morse ran with his ideas. Further, Gale showed Morse how to use electrical relays to extend the distance that signals could carry.

Meantime, skilled technician Alfred Vail refined the telegraph key used to send messages. Vail also played a major role in devising the dot-and-dash code, and managed construction of the initial telegraph lines.

In 1838, Morse and his team successfully transmitted signals across two miles of wiring at New Jersey's Speedwell Iron Works, a foundry owned by Vail's father. The message sent was rather prosaic: "A patient waiter is no loser."

Politically Charged Communications

Morse demonstrated his invention to President Van Buren and his aides. Indeed, for years Morse had urged Washington, in the interest of "wiring the country," to fund his experiments. In 1843, the

U.S. Senate passed, and President John Tyler signed, a last-minute appropriation of $30,000 toward that end.

Flush with cash, Morse set about building a 38-mile line between Baltimore and Washington, D.C. For help, he turned to a talented engineer, New York's Ezra Corning. Corning invented a plow that, in rapid sequence, dug up the earth, inserted a telegraph cable, and then covered up the hole. Unfortunately, the cable that was purchased had weak insulation, ruining the scheme. Time, and money, were running out. A worried Morse latched onto a brainstorm of Corning's: simply string the telegraph wire from posts and trees.

On May 1, 1844, the Whig political party convention in Baltimore nominated former Senator Henry Clay for president. From Annapolis Junction, midway between Baltimore and Washington, Vail transmitted news of the nomination along the newly strung line to the Capitol. There, his message was received hours before convention delegates made it back to the capital city.

Then on May 24, Morse sent a message from Baltimore's Mount Clair railway station to the chambers of the Supreme Court. Attendees listened with rapt attention as the noble-sounding text, taken from the Bible, was read aloud: "What God hath wrought." The verse was selected by Annie Ellsworth, the daughter of the head of the U.S. Patent Office, an early backer of Morse.

Telegraph Nation

With a new technology proven, telegraph lines exploded across America, following the path of rapidly expanding railroad lines. By 1854, the country had 23,000 miles of transmission wire. Thousands of ambitious men became telegraph operators, including a young Thomas Edison, who would conjure even greater electrical innovations. Some operators suffered from a now-typical malaise of the new "high-tech" field—repetitive motion injury—from tapping straight down on the telegraphy key. To prevent this ailment, tinkerers devised a swivel key.

Ezra Corning, meantime, founded Western Union, for several generations the main means by which Americans sent telegraph messages and kept in touch with business and family relations from far away. With the wealth generated by his company, Corning cofounded New York's Cornell University.

Apart from invention, Morse engaged in a frustrating, yearslong battle to secure the patent rights for his device. He wrote: "I have been so constantly under the necessity of watching the movements of the most unprincipled set of pirates I have ever known, that all my time has been occupied in defense, in putting evidence into something like legal shape that I am the inventor of the Electro-Magnetic Telegraph!!"

Finally, in 1853, Supreme Court Chief Justice Roger Taney ruled that Morse had been first in configuring a practical, working telegraph. Morse's personal wealth soared as telegraph companies paid him the rights to his device. The tenacious inventor gave away much of his money to institutions such as Yale and Vassar College. He died in 1872.

Since ancient times, mankind had been limited to sending messages by horse, ship, the lighting of fires, and the beating of drums. Yet by 1866, after the laying of the first transatlantic telegraph cable, people could even send messages across the oceans almost instantaneously. Grand variations on Morse's theme—telephone, radio, television, Internet, cell—would follow.

AMERICAN MUSIC:
KINGS OF SWING AND RHYTHM

I t was a stunning sight, and sound, for the "high brows" of Carnegie Hall, the classical-music venue of New York City, on January
16, 1938. The orchestra in question, although neatly attired, was not
playing Brahms, but Basie.

In fact, with songs like "I Got Rhythm," a series of acts were
providing a veritable history of jazz, the rhythmic, popular music
that in recent decades had been shaking up the country, and much
of the world.

ALL-STAR LINEUPS

There were African-American spirituals. And popular songs, fit
for a Broadway stage or a vaudeville hall, played and sung with a

rhythmic lilt. There were up-tempo "swing numbers" propelled by powerhouse drummer Gene Krupa, trumpeter Harry James, and other talented bandmates of the headliner, clarinetist Benny Goodman, the acclaimed "King of Swing." The audience members, far from listening politely, clapped loudly and stomped their feet.

The intense, exacting Goodman, born in 1909 and raised in Chicago, was the son of immigrants from the Russian provinces of Poland and Lithuania. From age 16, he had been playing with the likes of future jazz superstar Glenn Miller and trombonist Jack Teagarden. Along the way he was assisted by music impresario John Hammond—scion of the Vanderbilt railroad family—who would discover other jazz standouts like Billie Holiday and, much later, famed musicians of the rock-and-roll era.

In Chicago in 1935, Goodman put together the "first jazz concert," a sit-down affair as opposed to the usual dance hall shake-up. He also recruited pianist Teddy Wilson and vibraphonist Lionel Hampton, both of African-American ancestry, thus breaking the "color line" in music a dozen years before Brooklyn Dodgers player Jackie Robinson did so in baseball. His band, with arrangements from Fletcher Henderson, developed a distinctive style of "swing," the brassy, big-city sound that had supplanted the New Orleans–based "Dixieland jazz" of Louis Armstrong. Goodman, pushed by Hammond, would later add soloist Charlie Christian, playing the novel instrument of the electrified guitar, destined to have a vast impact on pop music. Flush with success, Goodman's outfit was booked on a nationally syndicated, late-night CBS radio show.

However, the nationwide tour that followed was disappointing. When his band arrived in Los Angeles in summer 1935, for a concert at the 21,000-seat Palomar Ballroom, a glum Goodman was ready to retire from the spotlights. But unbeknownst to him, many young jazz lovers in California had listened to his radio concerts, broadcast three hours earlier on the West Coast, early enough for the youths to stay up late.

Meantime a new kind of promoter, the radio "disc jockey," had been trumpeting his work. The result was "bandemonium," as throngs of teenagers surged toward the Palomar's stage, hoofing wildly to Goodman's sound. This prefigured the masses of crazed youths that would swoon and obsess over jazz singer Frank Sinatra in the 1940s, Elvis Presley in the 1950s, the Beatles on their tours of the U.S. in the 1960s, song-and-moon-dance man Michael Jackson in the 1980s, and innumerable other wildly popular "rhythm acts."

Novelty within the Tradition

What Goodman was doing was unique, but also of a piece with American musical trends before and since. Performers take European instruments, like woodwinds, brass, and drums, and the old continent's musical forms, like classical and church music. Then they add American musical styles, be it Stephen Foster's folk songs of the 1850s, the catchy Broadway and Tin Pan Alley tunes of the urban North, John Philip Sousa's marching-band stomps, the bluegrass of Appalachia, or blues or gospel permeating the postbellum South, or a banjo plucked from Africa. Finally they commercialize the music enough to reach the masses, via the ever-changing technology of the day: bandstands, recorded media, the airwaves, cassette tapes, and Internet downloads.

The formula has worked spectacularly again and again: Scott Joplin's syncopated ragtime of the early 1900s; the rap and hip-hop of the 1970s to today, using antiquated turntables and cutting-edge "sampling" technology to call up old-school hits to construct trendy new sounds; Hank Williams' music of the 1950s, broadcast on new-fangled television and featuring the new instrument of pedal steel guitar, borrowed from American Hawaii; and so forth.

Goodman himself went full circle, back to his European roots. After having calluses surgically removed from his fingers, and building stronger jaw muscles through endless practice, he recorded a series of symphonic albums on classical clarinet.

But he's remembered mostly for a strange new sound that's echoed down the eras: the stomping of feet at the venerable Carnegie Hall.

NATIONAL DEBT:
IN THE RED

By 2011, the U.S. government carried a national debt of $14 trillion, and faced $46 trillion in future obligations for federal "entitlement" programs such as Medicare and Social Security.

In starting out, the federal government had a fair amount of public debt, after it took on state government and private costs incurred during the American Revolution. Into the early twentieth century, this so-called national debt had usually been modest, and had generally declined in amount, with the major exception of the Civil War. In more recent times, given the two world wars, the Great Depression, and the Recession of 2008, it has more often been substantial and on the rise.

Paying What's Owed

The first national administration of President George Washington, at the urging of the financially adept Treasury Secretary Alexander Hamilton, assumed the $75 million in obligations the nation had accumulated during the Revolution. The gross domestic product, or GDP, of America in 1790 amounted to about $190 million. Thus the national debt was equivalent to about 40 percent of the total of all the country's goods and services at that time.

This debt, even with the additional obligations acquired under the Louisiana Purchase, was steadily paid off for several decades. Then the costs of the unexpectedly long and bloody War of 1812 pushed the debt back up to $125 million. Yet this was only about 13 percent of a GDP that had risen to $960 million.

The national debt actually disappeared during the administration of the premier "deficit hawk," President Andrew Jackson. Born poor, and burned by personal debts, Jackson had a horror of banks and financial obligations. On taking office in 1829, he faced a national debt of about $50 million. Over two terms Jackson piled up surpluses and quashed expensive spending bills for "internal improvements"—road and canal building that would be called "infrastructure projects" today. By 1835, his Treasury Department was $450,000 in the black. Jackson noted: "How gratifying the effect of presenting to the world the sublime spectacle of a Republic of more than 12 million happy people free from debt!"

Ups and Downs

However, deficits and debt roared back in 1836, with a severe economic downturn. They've been with us ever since. Some historians blame Jackson's stingy tightening of credit for that recession. As in 2008, though, an asset bubble triggered by overheated speculation in real estate contributed to the red ink.

By 1860, the national debt was quite a small amount, $65 million, 1.5 percent of a GDP of $4.35 billion. Then, with the Civil War, federal debt soared to previously unheard-of totals, $2.7 billion soon after the war, though still just about one third of the GDP.

After a long period of rapid growth, and steady paying off of the Civil War debt, new obligations were incurred with the Spanish-American War. The major fighting in that 1898 conflict only lasted four months, however, and balanced budgets and debt pay-downs followed in the generally prosperous years up to 1917, with the U.S. entry into the First World War. By 1919, when that bloody and expensive war was over, the debt stood again at about a third of the GDP.

During the Roaring Twenties' boom, budgets were often balanced, as they have been—surprisingly from our perspective—for most years in American history. Then the Great Depression of the 1930s brought in "Keynesian economics," whereby large-scale spending and large deficits were employed in an attempt to spur the economy. The national debt rose to 45 percent of the GDP by the late 1930s. It kept going up, fast, in the 1940s during the Second World War. The national debt, $16 billion in 1930, at the start of the Depression, was $260 billion in 1950, five years after the war. As a proportion of the GDP, the debt peaked in 1946, at 121 percent.

Mortgaging the Future?

Debt as a proportion of the GDP steadily fell, to 56 percent in 1960, after the often-tight budgets, tax cuts, and prosperity of the Eisenhower years; then to 38 percent in 1970, after the Kennedy and Johnson Vietnam-era "guns" and Great Society–era "butter" of the prosperous 1960s; and to 33 percent in 1980, despite the twin oil-price-fueled recessions of the 1970s, which were punctuated by periods of growth.

During the following decade, the Reagan administration saw

marked rises in military and domestic expenditures, and the debt percentage rose to 56 percent. The Clinton era of the 1990s managed to run a budget surplus in 1998, and witnessed the debt percentage rise slightly, to 58 percent by 2000. Then, in the George W. Bush years up to 2007, the debt percentage rose appreciably to 66 percent. Sharply higher domestic and military spending followed the late-1990s Internet bubble collapse and September 11th terrorist attacks, and subsequent recession.

After a period of growth, the banking crisis of 2008 touched off a severe recession, and massive spending. The national debt ascended quickly, reaching in 2011 $14.5 trillion, a proportion to the GDP of about 100 percent, the highest since the Second World War, with tens of trillions more owed for future social program payments.

If history is a good judge, the speed with which the U.S. pays off this debt will depend on how rapidly its economy expands. The fast debt run-ups of the Revolutionary War, Civil War, First World War, and the Great Depression/Second World War were all followed by sustained periods of growth and rising private-sector profits and governmental revenues that served to pay down the accumulated deficits.

Like a prosperous family able to pay off its mortgage and car payments, if its purchases are held to a reasonable level, the U.S. will hopefully once again grow its way out of what it owes.

The National Parks:
Yosemite and Beyond

The extensive array of U.S. national parks sets aside for all time, for all to visit, at little cost, the nation's most scenic and historic sites and monuments, including the Grand Canyon, Little Bighorn Battlefield, and the White House.

The notion of preserving America's special lands dates to George Catlin, a painter of Native Americans in their natural settings. In 1832, Catlin called for a preserve of American Indian territory stretching from Canada to Mexico.

Yosemite and Yellowstone Fire the Imagination

By 1855, travelers had witnessed the splendor of California's Yosemite Valley, and its Mariposa grove of 275-foot tall sequoia trees.

In 1864, U.S. Sen. John Conness of California introduced a bill to set aside, for the state of California, 60 acres of the region for "public use, resort, and recreation." President Lincoln ceded federal land for this novel state park.

By the early 1870s, expeditions to Wyoming's Yellowstone River confirmed rumors of a region of fantastic geysers and roiling "mud pots." Boosters of the Northern Pacific Railroad, such as Nathaniel Langford, sought to increase travel to the area, and bankrolled some of these early treks. In March 1872, President Ulysses S. Grant established Yellowstone as the first national park in America, and the world.

At first, the two-million-acre Yellowstone National Park was poorly managed. Poachers decimated much of its buffalo and mule deer. *Field and Stream* editor George Bird Grinnell, founder of the Audubon Society, campaigned against these depredations. Then the cavalry rode to the rescue, in the guise of Gen. Philip Sheridan, the former Civil War commander. In 1886, Sheridan ordered cavalry Troop M to take control of the park. The army managed Yellowstone for three decades.

The cavalry also entered the fray near Yosemite, in areas marked by overgrazing and by logging of sequoia. Naturalist John Muir crusaded for a Yosemite National Park, which President Benjamin Harrison approved in 1890. Taking command of the rugged reservation was the Black Ninth Calvary Regiment, the "Buffalo Soldiers." Troopers sported peaked hats that, during the 1898 Spanish-American War, drained away the heavy downpours of their Cuban battlefields. Park rangers adopted their distinctive headgear.

MULE TEAMS, AND AN EXAMPLE FOR THE WORLD

The push for a truly national system of reserved lands was spearheaded by Stephen Mather, a marketing executive for the Pacific Coast Borax Company. Mather had cloaked the firm's cleansing product in Wild West gauze, with ad copy about Twenty Mule Team Borax. Disturbed at the parks' poor condition, he pushed laws permitting wealthy individuals like railway magnate Louis Hill to make large grants for park improvements. Mather also backed the "See America First" campaign of Hill's Great Northern Railway, which boosted tourist traffic to destinations like Montana's new Glacier National Park. In 1916, when the National Park Service was founded, Mather was made director.

The National Park System now consists of 391 separate sites and 84 million acres. A model for parks everywhere, it hosts 270 million visitors a year. It was and is a novel notion, that sprung from a very democratic ideal: take a country's most splendiferous sites, and reserve them for the enjoyment of the people.

FREDERICK LAW OLMSTEAD:
COUNTRY IN THE CITY

Millions have visited the unique rural expanse, bracketed by sky-scrapers, of New York's Central Park. Or the much-admired park systems of Louisville, Kentucky, or Buffalo, New York. Or Boston's "emerald necklace" of interlinked parks such as the Back Bay Fens, Jamaica Pond, and the Arnold Arboretum. Yet urban parks did not arrive in still largely rustic America until the 1850s. The notion of city parks, and the design of the above locales, were largely the work of one farsighted man—Frederic Law Olmstead.

Olmstead's father, a successful dry goods merchant from a seventh-generation Hartford, Connecticut family, often took his family on carriage "tours in search of the picturesque" throughout New England and northern New York. The younger Olmstead studied surveying and engineering, but sumac poisoning weakened his eyes and cut short his Yale college days. So he labored as a deckhand on a China-bound ship, where he came down with scurvy. Then, over seven years, he experimented with exotic trees on a Staten Island, New York orchard.

A COMMONS TO EDIFY THE COMMON FOLK

In 1850, Olmstead and his brother took a six-month hiking tour of Britain and the continent. At Birkenhead, a public park designed by English gardener Joseph Paxton, Olmstead was struck by how "art had been employed to obtain from nature so much beauty." He began to view public parks as a way of nudging America from a frontier culture to a more sophisticated civilization.

Helped by friends like Washington Irving, of Rip Van Winkle fame, Olmstead became construction chief and head architect for Central Park. Out of 33 bidders, he won the contract to design the place through mock-ups sporting the photographs of Mathew Brady, later famous for his Civil War images. Olmstead, along with state lawmakers and his business partner, architect Calvert Vaux, envisioned the 770-acre park as a kind of upper-class model for workers and immigrants. "Hundreds of thousands of tired workers," Olmstead wrote, "who have no opportunity to spend their summers in the country, [will have] a specimen of God's handiwork that shall be to them, inexpensively, what a month or two in the White Mountains or the Adirondacks is, at great cost, to" the wealthy.

Yet the envisioned paradise was then a public dump, "steeped in the overflow and mush of pigsties, slaughterhouses and bone-boiling works," Olmstead noted. He put 3,000 laborers to work planting over four million shrubs and trees, after they hauled out 10 million cartloads of dirt and stone.

The Civil War interrupted his landscape designs. As head of

the U.S. Sanitary Commission, Olmstead managed the medical supplies of the Union army's volunteers. His tattered fleet of steamships picked up and nursed wounded soldiers back to health.

Far-Flung Designs

In time Olmstead finished his great park, and founded the first full-time landscape architecture firm. He went on to design some 500 parks, suburban tracts, and university campuses. His commissions included: the U.S. Capitol grounds, Milwaukee's park system, Yosemite's Mariposa Tree Grove, the 1893 Chicago World's Fair, Brooklyn's spacious Prospect Park, the Stanford University campus, North Carolina's Biltmore Estate, and the walking paths about Niagara Falls. Olmstead applied his notions to transportation, inventing the "parkway"—a greenway for carriages, and later cars, which linked together parks throughout an urban area.

When Alzheimer's forced his retirement in 1895, the father of landscape architecture entered Massachusetts' McLean Hospital, whose grounds he had laid out. His friend, noted architect Daniel Burnham, eulogized: "He paints with lakes and wooded slopes; with lawns and banks and forest covered hills."

THE PANAMA CANAL:
BETWEEN PACIFIC AND ATLANTIC

Ferdinand Marie de Lesseps, the French mastermind behind the 1869 construction of Egypt's Suez Canal, had met his match. In Panama, a province of the Latin American country of Colombia, his firm had attempted to construct a 51-mile canal between the Atlantic and Pacific Oceans. In 1888, after seven years of excavating through jungle and swamp, and the deaths of 22,000 laborers, Lesseps' company had gone bankrupt.

SPEAK FORCEFULLY, AND CARRY A BIG SPADE

Enter an up-and-coming United States, and its aggressive young president, Theodore Roosevelt. In 1898, during the Spanish-

American War's Cuban campaign, Roosevelt had taken note when the USS *Oregon* took 66 days to steam from San Francisco to duty on the East Coast. To Roosevelt, a canal across Panama was vital to protect U.S. interests in Latin America and the Caribbean.

Roosevelt sent his secretary of state, John Hay, formerly Abraham Lincoln's private secretary, to negotiate a treaty with Colombia allowing the U.S. to build a canal in Panama. But the Colombian Senate rejected the pact. So Roosevelt's administration, with the help of Lesseps' former chief engineer, Phillippe-Jean Bunau-Varilla, backed a group of rebel Panamanians seeking independence. When their revolt broke out in 1903, the U.S. Navy blocked Colombia from sending in troops, and paid other Colombian troops to stay put.

Two weeks after gaining independence, the Panamanian government signed the Hay-Bunau-Varilla Treaty. In exchange for $10 million and yearly fees, Panama permitted the U.S. to build a 10-mile-wide canal. The U.S. later compensated Colombia with $25 million.

The First to Control Yellow Fever

The American canal project was led by the Army Corps of Engineers and the Army Medical Corps. The latter made medical history by alleviating diseases that had crippled the previous French attempt at creating the canal.

During the Spanish-American War in Cuba, U.S. Army Major Dr. Walter Reed had confirmed that yellow fever, endemic there and in Panama, was transmitted by mosquitoes. In the newly established Canal Zone, Reed's protégé, Surgeon Major William Gorgas, managed an intensive campaign to fight the disease-bearing insects, also the vector for spreading malaria. Gorgas and his men drained swamps, mowed down bug-breeding thickets, and replaced open windows with $90,000 worth of mesh screens. After 1906, the malarial death rate among workers dropped 90 percent, and sickness from yellow fever plummeted as well.

Construction, begun in 1904, was headed by engineer John Stevens, who'd supervised the building of the Great Northern Railroad through the Northwest Rockies. Stevens and his able successor, Army engineer Lieutenant Colonel Thomas Goethals, threw a hundred giant Bucyrus steam-powered shovels into digging the watery channels. By 1907, the project was excavating half a million cubic yards of soil per month, hauled away by 160 locomotives.

Moving Mountains

Their labor force consisted mainly of West Indian blacks, paid about a dollar a day. Stevens insisted on providing the workers with barracks, running water, churches, and schools. Still, some 5,600 laborers died during the project.

A major geological problem was soil made up of clay and iron pyrites. The iron, when exposed to air by digging, oxidized and weakened the rocks, which along with the soft clay led to continual landslides, sometimes burying workers alive, or blocking the canal. The biggest land obstacle was the mountain-like Culebra Cut; there, 40,000 laborers and 4,500 tons of dynamite were employed to hew and blast out a passage.

Rejecting Lesseps' plan for a level cut through the Panamanian countryside, Stevens approved a series of massive locks to raise ships along the canal. One set of locks was 350 yards long with walls reaching almost 50 feet high. Supplying the water for the locks was the 1.5-mile-long Gatun Dam, which hemmed up the formerly wild Chagres River. The mammoth dam was comprised of double walls of excavated stone and clay, 22 million cubic yards worth, which hardened into material impervious to watery assault. No electricity was needed for the locks, which operated entirely by the gravity-aided flow of water from the dam to the locks, then down to the oceans.

By August 1914, the Panama Canal was finished. The transoceanic passage slashed the distance for a New York to San Francisco voyage from 14,000 miles to 5,900. By the 1920s, about 5,000 ships a year were using the canal.

On December 31, 1999, possession of the Canal Zone reverted to Panama. But, as Roosevelt had envisioned, it had served as a vital transit point for U.S. warships and transport vessels during the First and Second World Wars. And its construction was an astonishing feat of engineering.

EDGAR ALLAN POE:
CREATOR OF LITERARY GENRES

The aisles of many contemporary book stores have sprawling sections dedicated to the edgy genres of fantasy, horror, science-fiction, and detective stories. The creator of these off-center and hugely popular genres lived an offbeat and tragic life of his own.

Born in Boston in 1809, Edgar Poe lost his actress mother to tuberculosis when he was under two years old. His father, David Poe, had abandoned the family the year before. The orphaned boy was taken in by wealthy Richmond, Virginia merchant John Allan, who lent Poe his middle name.

A NIGHTMARISH CAREER

Evincing an early talent for theatrics and classical literature, Poe enrolled in 1826 at the fledgling, chaotically administered University of Virginia. To Allan's rage, Poe ran up gambling debts and departed the school.

The slightly built, shy-seeming youth then, rather improbably, enrolled in the army, and rose to sergeant of artillery. Yet this was followed by an unhappy tenure as a cadet at the U.S. Military Academy at West Point. In 1831, Poe willfully brought on his own court martial and dismissal "for refusing to attend formations, classes, or church."

Poe's literary life followed a similar path of turmoil, as he proceeded from one editorial position to another, often after being ousted. A manic depressive, he started a failed literary magazine, and was dismissed from another, the *Southern Literary Messenger*, after he'd made it into a success. Desperately poor, in 1843 he sought a political office with the administration of President John Tyler, but showed up inebriated at the job interview. In the mid-1840s he achieved fame in America and Europe for his beguiling poem "The Raven." Yet he earned only $9 for the work, alienated expectant fans by giving a desultory public lecture, and angered fellow writers by accusing fellow poet Henry Wadsworth Longfellow of plagiarism.

In 1836, Poe had secretly married his 13-year-old cousin Virginia Clemm. She died in 1847. On October 7, 1849, Poe was found prostrate "in great distress" on a Baltimore street, and died the following morning. The cause of death has been variously attributed to epilepsy, rabies, a heart condition, drugs, or cholera.

New Forms of Narration

Yet over the course of a chaotic life, this troubled genius had created new forms of literature. Along with Mary Shelley, author of *Frankenstein*, he originated the horror and gothic genres. No one before had written such terrifying prose, such as "The Cask of Amontillado," in which the vengeful protagonist walls up a purported enemy inside a dank cellar, or "The Tell-Tale Heart," in which the narrator is driven mad by the pounding of his own pulse. Fascinated by phrenology—a pseudoscience that tried linking mental activities to different areas of the brain—Poe became a master of describing a character's inner psychology.

With tales such as "The Balloon Hoax," Poe was one of the first to write science fiction and fantasy about the emerging technologies of the day. Frenchman Jules Verne, the first widely popular science fiction writer, penned a follow-up to Poe's only novel, *The Narrative of Arthur Gordon Pym of Nantucket*.

Poe's character Auguste Dupin, the detective who solves "The Murders in the Rue Morgue" and other mysteries, was the prototype for Sherlock Holmes and innumerable other fictional detectives. British author Arthur Conan Doyle, the creator of Holmes, said of Poe: "Each of his detective stories is a root from which a whole literature has developed." In the investigatory tale "The Gold-Bug," Poe introduced the subject of cryptography, or ciphering. Reading this story inspired William Friedman, the Second World War's decipherer of Japan's secret military codes, to enter the cryptographic field.

The noted author of sonorous verse like "The Raven" and "Annabel Lee," Poe was also a renowned literary critic. And he was severely criticized by some writers. Poet Ralph Waldo Emerson termed Poe "the jingle man," and novelist Henry James claimed that "an enthusiasm for Poe is the mark of a decidedly primitive stage of reflection." More have been laudatory, like Boston poet James Russell Lowell. He termed his fellow scribe the "most discriminating, philosophical, and fearless critic upon imaginative works who has written in America."

JAMES K. POLK:
UNDERRATED CHIEF EXECUTIVE

Public opinion surveys often ask Americans to rank the greatest presidents. The names George Washington, Abraham Lincoln, Franklin Roosevelt, and, more recently, Bill Clinton and Ronald Reagan, often land near the top of these popular lists. Much less known is James Knox Polk, an overlooked one-term president who was intent on accomplishing a few big aims. He achieved them all, and made the U.S. a continent-wide power stretching from the Atlantic to the Pacific.

TOUGH, SMART, AMBITIOUS

A sometimes sickly, yet beguiling and intensely focused man, Polk, born in North Carolina in 1795, rose quickly to political power, after overcoming a terrible childhood illness. Diagnosed with bladder stones, at age 16 he endured surgery to remove the stones without anesthesia or antiseptic, brandy the only palliative.

His father was a prosperous Tennessee plantation owner, and his mother a descendant of Scottish Presbyterian reformer John Knox. Polk attended the University of North Carolina, where he was president of the Dialectic Society, or debating club. In Tennessee, he practiced law, and in his first case successfully defended his hot-tempered father from a charge of public brawling.

A supporter of fellow Democrat President Andrew Jackson, Polk was elected governor of Tennessee, and Speaker of the U.S. House of Representatives. In 1844, when Jackson's vice president, New York's Martin Van Buren, was the favorite for his party's presidential nomination, Polk cleverly urged his supporters to back Van Buren. When the nomination convention deadlocked, Polk, the original "dark horse" underdog candidate, emerged as the compromise nominee.

His election campaign was dominated by the issues of Texas, which had won independence from Mexico and now sought to join the United States, and the Oregon Territory, which the U.S. and Britain both claimed. Polk eagerly called for annexing both. His opponent, Whig candidate Henry Clay of Kentucky, lost the election largely due to ambivalence about such expansion. In private, President-elect Polk pledged to focus on four concise goals: acquire California; acquire the Oregon Territory; set up an independent federal banking system; and cut an unpopular tariff on imported goods.

The Oregon Territory then stretched from present-day southern Oregon to present-day British Columbia, the latter a possession of Britain. The expanse included Idaho and parts of Montana. War hawks wanted all of it, up to the 54°, 40' parallel of latitude, demanding, "Fifty-Four Forty or Fight!" President Polk, while sounding bellicose in public, quietly cut a deal with British Foreign Secretary

Lord Aberdeen, and set the boundary at 49 degrees, the northern border of present-day Washington State.

South to the Rio Grande

In 1845, Polk's first year in office, Texas entered the Union. Mexico and the U.S. bitterly disputed the new state's border, which Mexico claimed was not the Rio Grande River, but the Nueces River to the north.

Beyond the big state of Texas, Polk was thinking bigger. He sent an envoy to Mexico with an offer to buy California and New Mexico for about $25 million, roughly $725 million in 2010 dollars. Mexico refused. In May 1846, after U.S. troops under future president Gen. Zachary Taylor crossed the Rio Grande and blockaded a Mexican port, Mexican troops entered Texas and killed 11 U.S. soldiers. Polk demanded a declaration of war, stating that Mexico had "invaded our territory and shed American blood upon the American soil."

During the bloody, three-year Mexican-American War, Americans won stunning military successes. In California, American settlers under Army officer John C. Fremont tossed out the Mexican garrison. In Mexico, an outnumbered army led by Gen. Taylor won battles at Monterey, Veracruz, and Buena Vista.

Attempting to short-circuit the fighting, the Polk Administration secretly arranged safe passage to Mexico City for Gen. Antonio de Santa Anna, Mexico's former dictator, who pledged on taking power to sell off California. After taking power, Santa Anna reneged, and attacked U.S. forces. But an army under Gen. Winfield Scott went on to seize the castle of Chapultepec and enter Mexico City, the "halls of Montezuma." Many were killed and wounded in this war, perhaps 50,000 on the Mexican side, and 17,435 on the American.

Although some in his party now wanted to annex all of Mexico, Polk was satisfied. He sent diplomat Nicolas Trist to Mexico City to negotiate. After ignoring an order from an impatient Polk to return home, Trist hammered out on his own the Treaty of Guadalupe Hidalgo. In return for $15 million, Mexico ceded California, Nevada, Utah, and portions of New Mexico, Arizona, Colorado, and Wyoming. It also acknowledged U.S. sovereignty in Texas down to the Rio Grande.

The ambitious Polk then had his ambassador in Madrid offer to buy Spain's colony of Cuba for $100 million. Spain declined.

Polk fulfilled his economic promises as well as his foreign policy ones. He slashed tariffs to very low rates. And he set up a new federal banking system that lasted until the creation of the Federal Reserve Bank in 1913. Both the U.S. Naval Academy and the Smithsonian Institution were also established during his administration.

A GRAND AND DISPUTED LEGACY

Worn out from his detailed management of the Mexican war and the other initiatives of his single, eventful term, Polk contracted cholera during a trip to New Orleans. He died in Nashville in June 1849, just three months after leaving office.

Polk was controversial then and has been ever since. In 1848 the House of Representatives censured him for starting the Mexican war. Future Civil War general Ulysses S. Grant called it "one of the most unjust ever waged by a stronger against a weaker nation. It was an instance of a republic following the bad example of European monarchies." Yet President Harry Truman termed Polk "a great president. Said what he intended to do and did it."

With the Oregon Territory and the Mexican Cession, Polk acquired a "second Louisiana Purchase," increasing the size of the U.S. by a third, and setting its western boundary firmly along the Pacific Ocean, fulfilling what some then termed America's "manifest destiny."

Quarterbacks and Knickerbockers:
The National Pastimes of Sports

Babe Ruth pointing nonchalantly to the fences before smacking a homer. The Vince Lombardi trophy, named for a coaching legend, and awarded to the winner of the Super Bowl. Michael Jordan, suspended in midair, poised for a winning shot. These are symbols of a competitive and sports-loving country, and icons of America's three best-known sports, first dreamed up over a century ago in the U.S. or the border provinces of Canada.

BALLS AND BATS

The origin of the peculiarly American sport of baseball, the "national pastime," keeps getting pushed back in time. Contrary to myth, Civil War General Abner Doubleday—a hero of Fort Sumter and Gettysburg in the Civil War—did not invent the game on a field at Cooperstown, New York, site of the game's present-day Hall of Fame. The first "official" game of baseball took place on June 19, 1846, in Hoboken, New Jersey, at Elysian Fields, surely a field of dreams; there the New York Nine trounced the Knickerbocker Club, 23-1. The game was organized by Alexander Cartwright, a banking clerk responsible for new rules like getting a hitter out by touching, or throwing to, a base. Previously, one would throw out a player by "plugging" him with a thrown ball, which often led to brawls.

A form of the sport was played as far back as 1823, when a New York City daily printed a reader's comment on the game: "I was last Saturday much pleased in witnessing a company of active young men playing the manly and athletic game of 'base ball' in Broadway." In 1791, records show, Pittsfield, Massachusetts, banned "baseball" from within batting distance of the fragile windows of its town hall. In 1777–78, at Gen. George Washington's Valley Forge military camp, soldiers played a game that involved running from one bag to another. Baseball evolved out of many children's games and adult sports, including British rounders, with its four bases and called balls, and English cricket, which features bats, tossed balls, and an infield and outfield.

In 1857, the Knickerbocker squad became part of the first amateur baseball league, which within ten years had over 400 clubs nationwide. The first professional team, the Cincinnati Red Stockings, was formed in 1869. In the twentieth century, as professional teams played winter ball in the Caribbean, baseball became a hit in Central America. Introduced into Japan around 1870 by an American professor at today's Tokyo University, baseball blossomed into a major sport following the U.S. occupation of Japan in 1945, when Japanese children took to the game played by American GIs.

PADS AND HELMETS

Many have noted that football—contemporary America's most popular spectator sport, and distinct from the futbol or soccer that is the world's most popular game—has martial aspects. Quarterbacks hurl "the long bomb," defenders "blitz" quarterbacks, and officials hoist yardage markers that look like Roman army insignia. Yet football was originally much bloodier than even today's smash-mouth game.

The sport originated from Britain's "mob football," a soccer-like joust where a ball was advanced by kicking, and by pummeling rivals. In America, the sport at first was basically a free-for-all scrum, so vicious that in 1861 Harvard banned it. A later variant—featuring an oblong ball and the touchdown, both introduced by Montreal's McGill University in the mid-1870s—was rooted in rugby.

The game got a major assist from Walter Camp, a standout Yale University athlete and coach. From 1878 to 1889, Camp haunted football's rules-making committees, where he proposed the line of scrimmage, four downs, the forward pass, and penalties for foul play. But the sport remained brutal.

In 1905, 18 football players were killed on the gridiron, 33 in 1908. Then President Theodore Roosevelt pressured the leading football colleges to outlaw gang tackling and other dangerous stunts. Severe injuries fell off. By 1920, the game went pro. Olympian and college football great Jim Thorpe served as first president of the American Professional Football Association, based in tough industrial cities like Pittsburgh and Canton, Ohio, now the site of the Football Hall of Fame.

Even early football takes a back seat in aggression to the original game of lacrosse, America's true indigenous sport. Its inventors, the American Indians, called it "the little brother of war," and played it to train for intertribal bloodlettings. The lacrosse stick, along with forwarding a ball, was wielded to mash an opponent. As in a military campaign, thousands of Indians played it for days across fields stretching for miles.

As with football, American colleges adopted lacrosse in the late 1800s. Also as with football, Montreal aided its fellow cross-border sports enthusiasts. The city's rule-setting Olympic Club defined the positions on the field, hardened the ball, and altered the lacrosse stick to make it better for catching and relaying the ball, not bashing an opponent. Yet the sport, with its reputation for attracting "rugged folks" willing to hit, and get hit, retains its manly edge.

JUMPERS AND HOOPS

Like the telephone—invented by a Canadian-turned-American, Alexander Graham Bell—the sport of basketball was created by Canadian-turned-American Dr. James Naismith. Born in 1861, and raised in Ontario, the young Naismith played a centuries-old game called "duck on a rock," where kids would knock the stone off another rock with a high, arching shot from a distance of about 15 feet. Naismith studied theology and excelled at sports while a graduate student at the Canadian city and college most associated with U.S. sports—Montreal, and McGill.

In 1890, Naismith enrolled at the Young Men's Christian Association (YMCA) Training School in Springfield, Massachusetts, which today hosts the Basketball Hall of Fame. There Naismith was asked to create a "clean" indoor team game to keep students active during the winter months. Naismith minimized roughhouse play by having the players pass, not carry, the ball, and by placing the contended

goal on a wooden hoop high off the ground. To reach the goal, players needed a high, arcing shot like the kind Naismith recalled from
playing duck on a rock.

After inventing "hoops," Naismith got his medical degree, then
served as campus chaplain and basketball coach, from 1898 to 1938,
at the University of Kansas, a powerhouse of his new sport. By the
early twenty-first century, basketball was the rage from Indiana prairies to the inner city, and played by European pros and Olympic
athletes alike. And even American football was becoming popular
in some overseas lands, as the nation's indigenous sports drew in a
global following.

RELIGION IN AMERICA:
A MULTIPLICITY OF SECTS

While Europeans were introducing most of the New World's religious sects, they were settling religious scores in the Old World. In the 1640s, as newly arrived Puritans built up New England, back in England the Puritans, Protestant Anglicans, and Catholic Cavaliers fought a bloody civil war. At the same time, Protestants and Catholics in German-speaking lands—which would supply a huge wave of American immigrants—were fighting the Thirty Years' War. In the 1680s, French Catholics massacred Protestant Huguenots, with many survivors fleeing to America.

In Europe, religion was inextricably linked with politics, with kings and clerical authorities, and with official, state-sponsored faiths that often touched off distrust and oppression. In America, by contrast, a wide range of sects sprang up more or less free to operate as they saw fit. In so doing they largely sidestepped the Old World's bloodletting.

PROTESTANT INFLUX: PURITANS, EPISCOPALIANS, PRESBYTERIANS

Some of the original colonies did formally acknowledge the pre-eminence of the Church of England, a Protestant branch of Christianity established by King Henry VIII. The religion's followers, known as Anglicans, were renamed Episcopalians after the American Revolution's break with England. Many of the most prominent Americans, such as George Washington, have been Episcopalians, a generally wealthy and well-established group. But even in colonial times, Anglicanism was not completely dominant.

An important exception was New England's Puritans, or Congregationalists. They were Calvinists, followers of theologian John Calvin's stern, Biblically centered creed. Seeking religious liberty, the Puritans left England for the Netherlands, and then the English colony of Massachusetts. With their successful establishment of a "dissident" theology, and stress on free public schools, the Puritans were to have a major impact on American politics and education.

The Puritans' own sometimes intolerant approach to religious dissidents led to the founding of the nearby Rhode Island colony by Protestant preacher Roger Williams in 1636–37. Williams set up the first Baptist congregation in America, a denomination which became one of the country's largest.

Calvinist Presbyterians of Scotch-Irish heritage, meantime, came to settle much of Appalachia and the upland South, lending their fiercely independent outlook to those realms. Another important Southern religious group was African Americans, who fused

European religious forms with African cultural traditions. Over time this led to institutions like the Southern black Baptist church and Southern-American gospel music.

In 1624 the largely Calvinist Dutch established the colony of New Amsterdam, renamed New York after the British took control in 1674. From its early decades, the thriving seaport tended to attract faiths and ethnicities of various kinds.

In the eighteenth and nineteenth centuries, a great many German-speaking immigrants, many of them Lutheran Protestants, the so-called "Pennsylvania Dutch," settled much of Pennsylvania and adjoining colonies. Smaller Swiss, German-speaking sects such as the Amish, with their aversion to modern, non-Biblical ways, were also attracted to these areas. Pennsylvania itself was founded by the Religious Society of Friends, or Quakers, a Non-Conformist Christian sect that stressed pacifism. Nearby, the colony of Maryland was unique for its founding by Catholics.

Catholics, and Everyone Else

With these kinds of precedents, it was inevitable that religion in America, unlike the more homogeneous European states, would continue to develop with a multiplicity of sects. In much of nineteenth-century Europe, Mormonism, a religion with a sharply different scripture than other Christian faiths, would likely have been suppressed. In America, after much turmoil and journeying, the Mormons set up their own communities in Utah. In 1848, with the new territory won in the Mexican-American War, the U.S. incorporated in its Southwest a large population of Hispanic Catholics.

In the 1840s, after failed political revolutions in Europe and the potato blight in Ireland, millions from northern Europe, including many Irish Catholics, immigrated to the U.S. in search of liberty and economic opportunity. In the late nineteenth century, vast numbers of East European Jews, and Polish and Italian Catholics, among others, followed.

More recently, America has witnessed an influx of East Indian Hindus and Sikhs, Middle Eastern and South Asian Muslims, African evangelicals, and countless other groups of varying degrees of faith.

It seems no accident that, in the early twenty-first century, the U.S. remained, among technically advanced nations, the most religious, with upwards of 90 percent of the population evincing a belief in God. Unlike the official religions of Europe, discredited by their association with often oppressive regimes, religion in America has been largely free. It has flourished in this country largely as a result.

John D. Rockefeller:
King of Industry, Controversy, and Philanthropy

He was America's richest man ever. His ruthlessly efficient businesses were in the midst of the booming oil, railroad, and steel industries that, in the late 1800s, made America an economic colossus. His hard-edged success engendered great public distrust, and an "antitrust" movement that broke up his vast holdings. And he gave more money to charities, adjusted for inflation, than anyone in history, curing diseases, uplifting education, helping invent modern philanthropy.

John Davison Rockefeller was a son who rebelled against father while following the counsel of mom. His father, William, "Devil Bill," from upstate New York, was a much-traveled bigamist and con artist who hawked medical elixirs. His mother was a prim, devout Baptist.

A FURIOUS ASCENT TO THE TOP

The son's rise was swift and brilliantly executed. As a boy he made money by saving cash from chores, then making small loans to neighbors at 7 percent interest. His family moved to Cleveland, Ohio, where at age 16 he worked keeping books and collecting bills for a merchant shipper. Able to swiftly make complex calculations in his head, he was soon putting together complex deals on moving produce by canal and rail. At 19, he formed a partnership with a produce merchant firm; within a year, it had revenues of over $400,000. At the same time, Rockefeller gave 10 percent of his earnings to the Baptist church or other charities. Working tirelessly, he never smoked nor drank.

He realized Cleveland stood to benefit from its position straddling railroads that fed off the booming oil fields discovered in 1859 near Titusville, Pennsylvania. With supplies of whale oil dwindling, industry needed petroleum for byproducts like kerosene, to light businesses and homes. In 1863, Rockefeller formed an oil refining firm with his brother William.

Following his mother's dictum that "willful waste makes woeful want," he rapidly built a huge company that was a model of efficiency and self-sufficiency. It controlled every step of production, by owning its refineries, making its own oil barrels, oil tanks, and warehouses for storage, and supplying its own wagons and ships for transport.

The firm was the first to ship petroleum via oil tanks on rail cars, then the first to ship the stuff via pipelines. Oil prices plummeted, allowing millions to cheaply light their homes. Company chemists produced useful new distillates from the oil: naphtha, a component of paints, benzene as a cleaning substance, lubricants for machines, and the ointment petrolatum, later branded as Vaseline. Gasoline, previously discarded into lakes, and burned, was employed as an increasingly important fuel. The company paved the way for smog to replace horse droppings—the latter banished by railroad and auto—as the major city pollutant.

RUTHLESS COMPETITOR

Rockefeller dealt mercilessly with rival refiners. Typically he'd offer to buy a competitor for an above-market price. If it declined, he slashed prices and bought up its infrastructure and suppliers, and drove it out of business. At the same time, his partner, Henry Flagler, connived with railroads to get discount prices and rebates for shipments of petroleum, while charging rivals a premium, in effect taxing other companies to pay Rockefeller. Competition was wiped out—22 of 26 refiners in Cleveland alone, with most in Philadelphia and New York following suit.

By 1868, after five years of takeovers, Rockefeller ran the world's largest oil refiner. Renamed Standard Oil in 1870, it further exploded over the next 12 years into 41 corporations scattered over many states. In 1882, they consolidated into the Standard Oil Trust, run by nine trustees, dominated by the Rockefeller family, who picked the officers of each firm.

Dominant in oil, the company also entered the iron and steel trade, buying up much of Minnesota's metal-rich Missabe range, as well as a fleet of ore freighters. This ignited a brawl with steel tycoon Andrew Carnegie. This led to the properties' sale to banking and steel magnate J. P. Morgan who, like Carnegie, was leading Rockefeller-style consolidations of other industries.

TRUST TO ANTITRUST

By the 1890s, Rockefeller's Trust had over 100,000 employees, and owned 20,000 tanker cars and 5,000 oil wells in the U.S. alone. It had cornered 90 percent of the refining industry, and its distribution network supplied 80 percent of America's towns. In 1912, Rockefeller had a personal fortune of $900 million, worth 2.5 percent of U.S. output, about $100 billion in 2010 dollars, easily outpacing Warren Buffett.

Already fearful of its hardball tactics, the public grew angry at Standard Oil's bid to monopolize distribution of products to local "Mom and Pop" stores. States brought suit against the firm. Crusading "muckrakers," such as Ida Tarbell, author of the book *The Secret History of the Standard Oil Company,* and with her own father put out of business by Rockefeller, pilloried the Trust's shady merger and courtroom practices.

By the early 1900s, President Theodore Roosevelt was making use of the Sherman Antitrust Act to cut the trusts of various industries down to size. In 1911, the Supreme Court ordered Standard Oil Trusts' biggest component, Standard Oil of New Jersey, busted into 34 firms. These companies made up a who's who of what became today's global oil sector: ExxonMobil, ConocoPhillips, BP, and Chevron.

By the time of its breakup, Standard Oil's market share had been much reduced by competition, foreign and domestic, as in the vast new oil finds of east Texas. Rockefeller himself, his health weakened by overwork, had long before retired, in 1897, at age 58.

FAMILY TREES AND PHILANTHROPY

Yet through his wife, Laura Spelman, and his son John D. Rockefeller, Jr., he started a family tree that bequeathed: Vice President

Nelson Rockefeller, Arkansas Gov. Winthrop Rockefeller, Chairman of Chase Manhattan Bank (now J. P. Morgan Chase) David Rockefeller, and West Virginia Sen. Jay Rockefeller.

In retiring from business, the tycoon—and regular Sunday school teacher—reinvented himself, and followed the concluding advice of preacher John Wesley: "Gain all you can, save all you can, and give all you can." He gave away $900 million to various charities and schools, and dimes and nickels to kids he came across.

His endowments set up the Rockefeller Foundation, and greatly expanded the University of Chicago, wiped out hookworm in the South, established the historic theme town of Williamsburg, Virginia, and paved the way for over 20 Nobel Prizes in the medical and scientific arts at what became Rockefeller University.

As in business, and igniting public broils, John D. succeeded grandly at giving. At his death in 1937, out of $1.5 billion garnered in his 97 years, he had only $27 million left.

DR. JONAS SALK:
ENDING THE BLIGHT OF POLIO

At the height of the 1950s "Baby Boom," millions of American parents were terrified by the growing epidemic of polio that was afflicting the nation's youth. Although medical science had eradicated many communicable diseases like yellow fever, the rate of poliomyelitis had risen by 1952 to 57,628 new cases a year. The viral infection could cause muscle-wasting paralysis, and death, and it especially targeted youths. Out of fear of infection, parents were pulling their children out of school or forbidding them from swimming pools.

Working 16-hour days to find a cure for the dread disease was Dr. Jonas Salk, the New York son of Russian-Jewish immigrants.

A MICROBIOLOGIST LEARNS HIS TRADE

By 1928, at age 14, Salk had graduated from a Queens, New York high school for exceptional students. Next, he flourished in the achievement-driven culture of the City College of New York, which in the 1930s and 1940s turned out eight future Nobel Prize winners. Salk earned his medical degree in 1939 at New York University (NYU), having made the elite Alpha Omega Alpha Society. His NYU mentor, virologist Dr. Thomas Francis, Jr., brought him to the University of Michigan's School of Public Health. During the Second World War, Francis and Salk came up with an influenza vaccine for the U.S. Army.

In 1947, Salk was made director of the Pittsburgh School of Medicine's Virus Research Lab. He built a lab from scratch with money from Pittsburgh's Mellon family. He began work on polio, funded by Basil O'Connor, president of the National Foundation for Infantile Paralysis (NFIP). NFIP, which wheelchair-bound President Franklin Roosevelt set up in 1938, was later renamed the March of Dimes.

Salk and his team of researchers managed to classify the 125 strains of the virus into three general types. Salk drew on the work of Harvard researcher John Enders, who devised a way to grow viruses like polio in large quantities for experimentation.

Until then, vaccines such as smallpox used a small amount of the infecting organism to trigger the body's immune response. But Salk's tests convinced him that a polio vaccine could use dead virus, a safer material. He created a means of applying formaldehyde to kill the organism while keeping the virus intact.

HIS OWN GUINEA PIG

In 1952, Salk tested his vaccine on polio patients: the antibodies in their blood increased. Then he announced: "I will be personally responsible for the vaccine"—and tested the vaccine on himself, his wife, his three children, and his researchers. None got polio, and all evidenced signs of immunity.

In 1954, the most complex test of a vaccine in history took place. Taking part were over 200,000 volunteers, 20,000 health officials and doctors, and more than 1,800,000 school children from the U.S., Canada, and Finland, the "Polio Pioneers." Francis designed and supervised the mass vaccinations of the children, aged six to nine. With success tantalizingly close, O'Connor took NFIP into debt to fund Salk's work, while tens of millions of Americans contributed dimes to the cause.

A scare occurred when 200 of those vaccinated came down with the disease, and 11 of these died. But it turned out they had all been injected with an errant batch of vaccine traced to a single manufacturer.

BANISHMENT OF A DREAD DISEASE

On April 12, 1955, Francis announced the results of the vaccinations to a hall packed with 150 reporters, while over 50,000 doctors across the nation watched via closed-circuit TV. The vaccine, he explained, safely prevented polio. Around the country, assembly line workers paused in silent tribute and ministers rang church bells.

Queried about patenting the Salk vaccine, its creator replied: "Would you patent the sun?" Salk declined a ticker tape parade in Manhattan; instead, New York created eight medical scholarships in his name.

Soon the whole nation had "gotten its shots." By 1957, the yearly number of polio cases fell to 5,894. The same year, an orally administered vaccine devised by University of Cincinnati pediatrician Albert Sabin was tested. By 1994, all of North and South America were designated "polio-free."

The scourge of children had been dealt a mortal blow.

SEQUOYAH:
THE ALPHABET AND THE TRAIL OF TEARS

Sequoyah had his revelation in central Alabama, at the 1812 battle of Horseshoe Bend, where the U.S. Army vanquished the Creek, or Muskogee, Indians. According to some records, the son of a Cherokee Indian princess and Nathaniel Gist, an officer of George Washington's, Sequoyah had fought on the side of the U.S. commander, Gen. Andrew Jackson. During the campaign, Sequoyah was struck by the advantage that literacy gave the white soldiers compared to the unschooled American-Indian warriors. The whites could send out explicit orders, read letters from family members, and write up battle reports.

Over the next decade Sequoyah worked to assemble an alphabet for his own Cherokee people, who inhabited parts of Georgia, North and South Carolina, and Tennessee. At first he tried creating an image for every word in Cherokee. Some of his tribesmen thought he was crazy, or even taking part in witchcraft. Later, by drawing on numbers and Roman letters, he developed an alphabet of 86 images, one for each spoken syllable of Cherokee. Thousands of Indians were soon able to read and write in their own tongue; by 1828 the first newspaper in the language, the *Cherokee Phoenix*, was in print.

Tribal Civilizations

It seemed no accident that the Cherokees were the first indigenous tribe anywhere to develop their own written language. One of the Southeast's Five Civilized Tribes—along with the Chickasaw, Choctaw, Creek, and Seminole—they had taken on many European customs. In their tribal region, Cherokees set up sawmills and ranches, raised corn for export abroad, constructed churches, and dressed in Western clothes. Some owned slaves. They even had a written constitution—modeled after the U.S. Constitution.

But by 1830, the outlook was very bad for the Civilized Tribes. A continuous stream of whites had encroached upon their land. That year, gold was discovered in Cherokee Georgia, leading to a new stampede of interlopers. Further, Congress approved and Andrew Jackson, now president, signed the Indian Removal Act. The law passed by one vote, despite opposition from frontiersman and Tennessee congressman Davy Crockett. It required the forced transfer of Indian tribes to west of the Mississippi.

Most Cherokees were against leaving. But in 1836 some in the tribe, convinced staying in the East was a doomed cause, signed the Treaty of New Echota. The Cherokees gave up their ancestral homeland in exchange for a shaky promise of $5 million and lands in Indian Territory, today's Oklahoma.

A FORCED AND FRIGHTFUL MARCH

In 1838 the U.S. Army sent in 7,000 troops to enforce the evacuation. Cherokees were herded into rude stockades while looters broke into their former homes. Noted a missionary: "They have been dragged from their houses, and encamped at the military posts . . . multitudes were allowed no time to take any thing with them except the clothes they had on."

From summer 1838 to spring 1839, 15 separate groups of Cherokees, 16,000 people in all, trekked to Oklahoma by steamboat, horse, and foot. The route was dubbed the "Trail of Tears," from the Cherokee word for "place where they cried." Food was scarce, the weather scorching hot or freezing cold, diseases like dysentery rampant. Recalled one Indian: "Long time we travel . . . People feel bad when they leave Old Nation. Womens make sad wails." Perhaps 4,000 perished along the way. Meanwhile, in Georgia, vandals destroyed the printing press for producing Sequoyah's script.

Years before, that warrior-linguist had trekked to the distant West and seized upon a new dream: crafting a universal language for every Native American tribe. To this end, he visited Indian bands along the Texas and Mexican border. He died in that region in 1843, symbol of a valiant bid to bridge the gap between two clashing cultures.

Back in Georgia, the gold veins which triggered the Trail of Tears soon ran out. Yet in Oklahoma, with fair justice, several of the displaced tribes ended up living atop mineral deposits that made them rich.

THE STAR-SPANGLED BANNER:
NATION'S EMBLEM AND NATIONAL ANTHEM

It was two years into the War of 1812, and the British were winning. Seeking vengeance for the American sack of their Canadian capital of York, the British had in August 1814 occupied Washington, D.C.—and burned down the Capitol, the Supreme Court, and the White House. Then, sailing unopposed with a powerful fleet up Chesapeake Bay, some 5,000 troops turned their attention to the important port city of Baltimore.

THE THREAD OF THE STORY

Earlier in the year, local American commanders anticipating an attack had ordered the crafting of a Great Garrison Flag for hoisting atop Baltimore's main bastion, Fort McHenry. The Fort's commander, Major George Armistead, wanted an emblem "so large that the British would have no difficulty seeing it from a distance."

General John S. Stricker and Commodore Joshua Barney contracted the work to Mary Pickersgill, a woman skilled in making signal flags for the many ships plying Baltimore's busy harbor. Pickersgill set to work on two banners: a smaller storm flag, and a 30-foot-by-42-foot flag, to be the largest battle emblem in the world.

Assisting the seamstress was a youthful team: her 13-year-old daughter, Caroline; an indentured servant of African descent, 13-year-old Grace Wisher; and Pickersgill's nieces, Margaret Young and Eliza Young, 15 and 13 years of age.

After seven weeks, and for a fee of $405.90, the flag was finished. It was made of cotton and of dyed English-wool bunting. It displayed, to represent each State in the Union, 15 white stars and 15 red and white stripes.

COMPOSING A BATTLE CRY

On September 13, the fleet of 19 British ships off Baltimore began flinging cannon shells and rockets at Fort McHenry. During the 25-hour bombardment, Francis Scott Key anxiously watched. Key, a prominent Washington attorney, had boarded one of the enemy ships to represent an American civilian imprisoned on board. The next dawn, peering across the waters at the bastion several miles away, he spied the Great Garrison Flag, barely visible but still fluttering over the fort. Its assault stymied, the British invasion fleet retreated.

"Then in that hour of deliverance and joyful triumph," recalled Key, "my heart spoke." A talented poet in his spare time, Key jotted down the opening stanza on the back of a letter. It read:

O say can you see, by the dawn's early light,
What so proudly we hail'd at the twilight's last gleaming,
Whose broad stripes and bright stars through the perilous fight
O'er the ramparts we watch'd were so gallantly streaming?
And the rocket's red glare, the bombs bursting in air,
Gave proof through the night that our flag was still there,
O say does that star-spangled banner yet wave
O'er the land of the free and the home of the brave?

After writing out the remaining verses, Key set the lyrics to an English tune, "To Anacreon in Heaven," the theme song of a London gentleman's club. Anacreon was an ancient Greek poet with a fondness for wine and women. The song went:

To Anacreon in Heaven, where he sat in full glee,
A few sons of harmony sent a petition,
That he their inspirer and patron would be;
When this answer arrived from the jolly old Grecian:
Voice, fiddle, and flute, no longer be mute,
I'll lend you my name and inspire you to boot
And besides I'll instruct you like me to entwine
The myrtle of Venus with Bacchus's vine.

Very popular in America, the song was lent to several patriotic tunes before Key's reworking of it, including "Adams and Liberty," and Key's own 1805 song, "When the Warrior Returns from the Battle Afar."

Hit Tune

By October 1814, over 16 newspapers along the East Coast had published Key's new anthem, originally titled, "The Defense of Fort

McHenry." By capturing the patriotic feelings stirred by the war and the British invasion and retreat, "The Star-Spangled Banner" was a smash hit. Its popularity grew during the Civil War, when it again fused patriotic ideals with the American flag. In the 1890s, the U.S. military required its playing during the raising and lowering of the colors. Over time, the song came to be regularly played at school commencements, sporting events, and other public gatherings. In 1931, Congress and President Hoover officially made it the national anthem.

The flag itself has had an up and down history. It was scarred by the Fort McHenry battle. The family of Major Armistead, which inherited the banner, cut out many pieces of it to give to relatives and friends. Due to this, the banner lost one of its stars, and shrunk to 30 feet by 34 feet. In 1912, Armistead's grandson, New York stockbroker Eben Appleton, donated the flag to the Smithsonian, with the request it always be displayed to the public.

Time, and the glare of camera flashes, further damaged the fabric. In 1998, Smithsonian curators undertook a multi-year restoration project. This painstaking task included the removal of 1.7 million stitches dating from 1914. Conservators employed such tools as electron microscopy, infrared imaging by a NASA scientist, and analysis of amino acid content by a New Zealand specialist. In 2008, it was back on public display, at a special new gallery of the Smithsonian's Museum of American History.

The Statue of Liberty:
Freedom's Symbol

It was a grand construction project that failed, but it helped inspire another that spectacularly succeeded. In 1869 French sculptor Frederic-Auguste Bartholdi was visiting Egypt, where his nation was undertaking, unsuccessfully, the first attempt to build the Suez Canal. At the canal's northern terminus, Bartholdi envisioned a fitting crown to the canal: a giant statue, modeled after the Roman goddess Libertas, hoisting to the heavens a light-filled torch. Work on the canal was suspended, and Bartholdi filed away his artistic inspiration.

His friend, French jurist Edouard de Laboulaye, was the author of a three-volume history of the United States, and would later write a biography of Benjamin Franklin. Active in the antislavery movement, he'd helped defend France's fragile democracy against the restoration of a monarchy. Laboulaye wanted to honor a fellow free-dom-loving democracy—America—and its 1876 centennial. Surely a statue would make a fitting tribute, and his associate Bartholdi had the perfect one in mind, for placement in New York Harbor.

FUND-RAISING, AND A FAMOUS ENGINEER

Both nations went to work raising money for the ambitious work of art. The U.S. collected money through plays, auctions, and boxing matches. After a dispute arose over the expense of the statue's pedestal, Congress rejected giving $100,000 for the statue, and New York Gov. Grover Cleveland vetoed a $50,000 appropriation. But Joseph Pulitzer, publisher of *The World* newspaper, and founder of the Pulitzer Prizes in journalism, gathered funds by printing in his publication the name of every contributor, even children donating from their piggy banks.

France raised $250,000, much of it through performances, at the Paris Opera, of "Liberty Enlightening the World." Later, in acknowl-edgement of France's grand gift, the U.S. would donate $10 million to various French charities.

To build the 151-foot-high figure, Bartholdi enlisted the help of a famous engineer, Alexandre Gustave Eiffel, who would later build the 1,063-foot Eiffel Tower in Paris. The statue they constructed had three layers. At its core, for support, was an enormous pylon of iron. Around this was a skeleton of steel, to let the top-most layer, a cop-per sheath, bend flexibly in the harbor's winds. The skeleton, from the interior perspective, looked rather like the spike of the future Eiffel Tower.

The exterior copper formed the figure of a Lady Liberty. Bar-tholdi's foundry hammered out the 62,000 pounds of metal into a patina just 1/32nd-of-an-inch thick. Later the sculptor of Mt. Rush-more, Gutzon Borglum, refitted the copper torch with window glass and interior lighting. In New York, workers built the statue's 154-foot base (including the pedestal). It was formed from 24,000 tons of concrete, the largest amount ever poured at that time. The 11-point, star-shaped base is from a fort that previously occupied the harbor site.

The dimensions of the statue were gigantic for the late nineteenth century, before the construction of skyscrapers. The figure stands 305 feet, comparable to a 30-story building, from the base of the pedestal to the top of its torch.

In France, the finished statue consisted of 352 pieces. Most were shipped for assembly from France to America in 214 crates. Others, such as the torch and the right arm, were sent beforehand, to raise funds at the centennial celebrations in Philadelphia. Then all the pieces were put back together again in New York.

Ticker Tapes and Huddled Masses

After many delays, Grover Cleveland, now president, dedicated the Statue of Liberty on October 28, 1886, before a large crowd at Bedloe's Island, renamed Liberty Island. Bartholdi had selected the location himself during a visit to New York, choosing it because of its dramatic position in the harbor. That day, a parade celebrating the statue marched past Wall Street, which, unlike the rest of the city, hadn't taken a holiday. To honor the procession, the brokerage houses' ticker tape boys rolled long strings of tape out their windows. The local tradition of ticker tape parades was thus born.

The statue's size and water location made it a natural lighthouse, and it served as one until 1902. It also famously served as a beacon of freedom for millions of immigrants entering New York through nearby Ellis Island. The Statue of Liberty was the first structure on American soil that passengers could see from an approaching ship. It is perhaps the most famous symbol of the United States.

Emma Lazarus, a descendant of immigrants, composed, as part of the fund-raising campaign for the statue, a well-known "huddled masses" poem of hope and freedom that is inscribed on the pedestal:

> *Give me your tired, your poor,*
> *Your huddled masses yearning to breathe free,*
> *The wretched refuse of your teeming shore;*
> *Send these, the homeless, tempest-tost to me,*
> *I lift my lamp beside the golden door!*

THE FIRST THANKSGIVINGS:
BOUNTY'S GRATITUDE

In the spring of 1621, the small band of Pilgrims struggling to survive at the Massachusetts Bay wilderness was astonished. They encountered an Indian named Tisquantum, whom the English settlers called Squanto, and who spoke the King's English.

PILGRIMS AND A WAYFARING INDIAN

Seven years prior, Tisquantum had been kidnapped by a rogue seaman serving under English adventurer John Smith, of Pocahontas fame. Hunt had sold Tisquantum into slavery, but the Indian had managed to make his way to England, where he'd served as an interpreter for the Newfoundland Company. After returning in 1620 to his native land, Tisquantum was positioned as a natural mediator between the settlers and Native Americans.

The Pilgrims were practitioners of a Puritan branch of Protestantism that dissented from the official Church of England. On the ship the *Mayflower,* they'd voyaged from Plymouth, England, to America, in search of religious freedom and property. They'd arrived in November 1620—after the growing season, and after a nine-week voyage that had left half of the 102 passengers dead from cold and disease. More had died since, as the Pilgrims shuttled back and forth, from *Mayflower* to shore, to build rude storehouses and scrape together what provisions they could.

THANKSGIVING IN MASSACHUSETTS

However, with the help of Tisquantum and other natives, they began to adapt to the new land. The English-speaking Indian helped them make peace with local tribesmen, including the powerful chieftain Massasoit. The Pilgrims also learned to grow corn, avoid poisonous plants, and draw sap from the maple tree. By the fall of 1621, they were no longer hungry, and had brought in a plentiful harvest.

The devout Pilgrims were accustomed to giving thanks to God for good times, while fasting in hard times. So their leader, Governor William Bradford, invited the Indians to a three-day feast of thanksgiving. Wrote Pilgrim Edward Winslow: "Our wheat did prove well, and God be praised, we had a good increase of Indian corn . . . Our harvest being gotten in . . . we might after a special manner rejoice together after we had gathered the fruit of our labors."

In 1623, after a drought, and a fast—followed by rains and an even better harvest—the Pilgrims put on an even bigger fête. Wrote Bradford, "For which mercy, in time convenient, they set apart a day of thanksgiving." Scrapping communal farming for individual plots of land also helped expand the harvest.

Along with venison, from deer supplied by the Indians, these first thanksgiving dinners included, Bradford recalled, a "great store of wild turkeys." The Pilgrims and Indians put on true feasts. They offered waterfowl; seafood, like cod, lobster, and clams; corn, barley, and wheat; chestnuts and walnuts; squash; fruit, like gooseberries and strawberries; and vegetables, like radishes, carrots, leeks, and onions.

THANKSGIVING IN VIRGINIA, AND THE NATION

Far to the south, meantime, the Colony of Virginia had already proclaimed its own thanksgiving. On December 4, 1619, 38 English landed on the James River near the existing settlement of Jamestown. As their charter stated: "We ordaine that the day of our [ships'] arrival at the place assigned for plantacon (plantation) in the land of Virginia shall be yearly and perpetually kept holy as a day of thanksgiving to Almighty God."

As the Massachusetts Bay Colony grew, formal offering of thanks became a yearly event. Other colonies, and later the states, picked up on the tradition. Then, in 1789, President George Washington issued a proclamation that did "recommend to the People of the United States a day of public thanksgiving and prayer." Its aim was to acknowledge the establishment of peace, prosperity, and the new "constitutions of government."

In the early nineteenth century, author Sarah Josepha Hale, known for writing "Mary Had a Little Lamb," campaigned to make Thanksgiving a formal national holiday. During the Civil War, President Abraham Lincoln obliged, making its date the last Thursday in November.

Thanksgiving has become a major holiday embracing all manner of things, particularly football watching, parades, and the start of a feverish shopping season. But its original spirit of gratitude lingers.

THE
TRANSCONTINENTAL RAILROAD:
TIES THAT BIND

On a rise in the Utah outback in May 1869, California Gov. Le-
land Stanford, representing the Central Pacific railroad, aimed
his hammer at the golden spike—and missed. Wild laughter broke
out among the champagne-guzzling crowd. Union Pacific president Thomas Durant next aimed at the railroad tie's spike—and also
missed. The throng of Irish and Chinese immigrant laborers, busi-
nessmen, politicians, and Civil War veterans erupted again. "It was a
very hilarious occasion," recalled one observer.

Finally, the spike was driven in, and telegraph operators sent
the momentous message: "DONE." Cannon blasts and tolling bells
of celebration rang out in distant cities. Two railways, starting from

different strands of the nation and laying track across every conceivable terrain, had met in the middle. The U.S. had its first transcontinental railroad, and its first speedy, reliable transportation across a vast continent.

Roots of the Rails

After 1848, the California Gold Rush brought a stream of settlers to the West Coast, as well as demand for faster transportation to get there. In 1861, Sacramento railroad engineer Theodore Judah led an expedition that discovered a practical west-east railway route, via the Donner Pass, from the Pacific through the Sierra Nevada Mountains.

When the Civil War erupted that year, the Northern states pushed through Congress a northern transcontinental route, which the seceding Southern states had previously blocked. On July 1, 1862, President Lincoln, once a railway lawyer, signed a Pacific Railroad bill. It granted two railroad companies 30-year loans, and ten square miles of adjacent land for each mile of track laid. A fee was set for each mile of rail: $16,000 in bonds for flat terrain, and up to $48,000 for construction in the mountains.

Central Pacific, starting in 1863, built tracks from Sacramento, heading east. Union Pacific, starting in 1865, headed westward from Council Bluffs, Iowa westward, through Nebraska and the Colorado, Wyoming, and Utah Territories.

Eastward through the Rockies

Central Pacific was run by a high-powered board that included mining supplier Collis Huntington; dry goods merchant and savvy construction supervisor Charles Crocker, later California's highest-ranking judge; and mining grocer Stanford, soon the state's governor.

For his 690 miles of track, Crocker hired upwards of 12,000

workers: track layers, stonecutters, smithies, surveyors, and engineers. He employed Irish immigrants, Mormons proffered by Utah Mormon leader Brigham Young and, for the most backbreaking work, laborers from China. Stanford objected to these "dregs from Asia," but Crocker, admiring their work ethic, responded: "Did they not build the Chinese Wall, the biggest piece of masonry in the world?" The Asians—paid about a dollar a day and living in bunkhouses and tents—at times made up 80 percent of the labor force.

The high Sierra Nevada was a daunting obstacle. Snowfalls and avalanches buried tracks and laborers, until carpenters fashioned large wooden sheds to shield the lines. Hand drilling was painfully slow, so explosives blasted out the rock. Yet the railroad's supplies of unstable nitroglycerin could blow up unexpectedly, once killing 15 at a Wells Fargo office in San Francisco. Then British chemist James Howden devised a means of making nitro on site. Workers were lowered in baskets by crane to carefully place the charges, then quickly hauled up before detonation.

WESTWARD TOWARDS THE COAST

The Union Pacific kicked off operations in 1865, after the war's end freed up former Union and Confederate soldiers for work. The company was led by Mississippi and Missouri Railroad owner Thomas Durant. During the war, Durant had made a pile smuggling contraband Southern cotton. He hired the skillful, hard-edged Grenville Dodge as his chief engineer. Dodge had maintained wartime rail lines for Union generals Ulysses S. Grant and William Sherman.

Durant, and later Massachusetts Rep. Oakes Ames—as president of Union Pacific's financial front company, Crédit Mobilier—handed out valuable railroad bonds to powerful politicians. These included future president James Garfield and future presidential nominee James G. Blaine. Meantime, Crédit Mobilier charged double rates for its construction work. In 1872, as Ames blew the whistle on his cronies, one of the worst scandals in American history would come to light.

Payoffs and profiteering aside, Dodge began laying out 1,087 miles of track through the prairie. With practice, gangs worked with precision: teamsters dropping off material from horse-drawn carts, burly rail workers rushing up 500-pound beams, gaugers ensuring the rails were aligned, bolters connecting them, shovelers leveling the rail beds with dirt. Yet some work was still shoddy. With both companies paid by the mile, they often rushed things when short of supplies, knocking in seven spikes when ten were required.

Another concern, on the Great Plains, were raids by American Indians, enraged by the iron road's encroachment. In 1867 a band of Cheyenne looted and killed the crew of a workmen's train. The lone survivor was found holding his own scalp. Union Pacific hired gunmen to shoot down the tribes' sustenance: buffalo. Undeterred, in 1868 Sioux leader Red Cloud became the only Native American to win a war with the U.S. military, forcing guarantees of his tribe's Bozeman Trail hunting lands. Other mayhem resulted from the "Hell on Wheels" towns of prostitutes, outlaws, and saloonkeepers that sprung up along the rails. In 1868, the Vigilance Committee of Laramie, Wyoming, restored order by stringing up criminals and gamblers from telegraph posts.

THE TIES THAT BIND

Finally, in 1869, the tracks of the two companies joined, at the drunken, gold-spiked ceremony that Stanford and Durant attended. The resulting regular train service from the Midwest to the Far West had profound consequences.

The Transcontinental Express train cut the journey from New York to San Francisco from months to just 83 hours. The expanse of the "Great American Desert" became populated with hundreds of thousands of settlers. The Indians who had roamed through such lands were largely consigned to reservations. Stanford, enriched by Central Pacific, endowed what would become Stanford University. And the Iron Horse supplanted the pioneer-filled wagon trains and Pony Express riders of the past.

UNITED FLIGHT 93:
HEROES OF 9-11

At 9:20 that crystal-clear morning, passengers were huddled in the back of a jetliner, making worried calls to friends and loved ones from 35,000 feet over eastern Ohio.

Tom Burnett, Jr., a 38-year-old father of three young daughters, called his wife Deena in California. "I'm on United Flight 93 from Newark," he told his spouse. "The plane has been hijacked."

Minutes before, near the front of the plane, three men had jumped up, brandishing knives and donning red bandanas. They rushed into the cockpit, disabling the pilot and first officer. A fourth man, the hijacking's leader, Ziad Jarrah, took over the controls. Speaking over the intercom, he claimed to have a bomb, and ordered the passengers to stay put.

A Diabolical Plan

The United hijacking was part of a plot masterminded by radical Islamic terrorists, most of them from Saudi Arabia. They aimed to seize U.S. airliners and steer them into important government and commercial buildings. The conspiracy was hatched by Osama bin Laden, the Afghanistan-based leader of the terror group al-Qaeda.

On that day, September 11, 2001, two groups of five hijackers seized two other airliners, both out of Boston's Logan International Airport, and flew them into New York's World Trade Center. They knocked the twin, 110-story towers to the ground, killing 2,750 people, including 343 firefighters.

Five other men hijacked American Airlines Flight 77, out of Washington Dulles International Airport, and flew it into the Pentagon, the Defense Department's headquarters in Arlington, Virginia. The aircraft severely damaged the west side of the building, and killed 184 persons.

The hijackers had entered the U.S. in 2000–2001, with some preparing for their attack by undergoing flight training in Florida, Arizona, and California.

The four hijackers aboard United Flight 93's Boeing 757 sought to fly their plane toward Washington, D.C., and crash it into either the Capitol or the White House.

An Awful Realization

Aboard the jetliner, passengers continued making calls. Burnett's wife informed him, "They're taking airplanes and hitting landmarks all up and down the East Coast." Other passengers received similar information. The awful realization took hold that their plane, too, was on a suicide mission.

Under the worst pressure imaginable, the passengers considered their options. Burnett told his wife: "Deena, if they're going to crash the plane into the ground . . . we can't wait for the authorities. We have to do something now."

The passengers took a vote. They decided to charge the cockpit, and try to take back control of the aircraft. The passengers grabbed hold of whatever makeshift weapons they could find. Then Todd Beamer—a 32-year-old father of two sons, his wife Lisa five months pregnant—cried out: "Let's roll!"

They Went Down Fighting

The plane's flight and voice recorders, and the outgoing phone calls, paint a picture of what occurred. The passengers rushed the cockpit, and tried forcing their way in.

From within the cockpit, Jarrah yelled, "They want to get in here!" To thwart the assault, he rolled the plane left and right, and violently pitched its nose up and down.

It is unclear whether the passengers actually broke into the cockpit, but it is known that their actions unnerved the terrorists.

Jarrah said to another hijacker, "Is that it? . . . Shall we put it down?"

"Yes . . . pull it down!" cried the other.

Realizing they would never make it to Washington, and shouting *"Allah Akbar!"*, Jarrah turned the plane onto its back, sending it into a steep dive.

At Shanksville, Pennsylvania, United Flight 93 smashed into the earth at 580 mph, igniting its 11,000 pounds of aviation fuel. All 44 on board were instantly killed. The aircraft was just 20 minutes from the capital.

By 2011, for the tenth-year anniversary, a National Park Service memorial to the doomed yet resolute passengers and crew was emerging in the Pennsylvania countryside at the site where their final flight crashed into the earth. The memorial contains a Tower of Voices, with 40 wind chimes, and a lengthy wall with 40 inscribed granite panels, both objects honoring each of those slain onboard.

Victory at New Orleans:
Old Hickory's Motley Crew

In December 1814, the British invaders of Louisiana had every advantage. They were supported by over 50 ships of the unbeatable Royal Navy. Their land force of roughly 8,000 professional soldiers had just helped defeat the mighty *Grand Armée* of Napoleonic France. In fact, its commander, Major General Pakenham, was the brother-in-law of Napoleon's conqueror, the Duke of Wellington.

Motley Crew

The defending American force was only half as big, and as motley as any ever fielded. It was made up of civilians from New Orleans, Choctaw Indians, former slaves called "free men of color," and Kentucky and Tennessee riflemen, all built around a U.S. Army regiment.

The War of 1812 was not going well. In August 1814, British invaders had sacked Washington, D.C. Now London sought to seize New Orleans and the rest of Louisiana, crippling America's coastal trade.

When the U.S. commander, Gen. Andrew Jackson, arrived in New Orleans on December 1, the city was close to panic from the approaching enemy host. And citizens of that sophisticated town, brought into the U.S. via the 1803 Louisiana Purchase, were unhappy at the behavior of the rough-hewn Americans. Some soldiers treated the city boulevards as latrines, while others were court-martialed for leaving sentry posts to sample the town's notorious homes of ill repute.

On December 12, a flotilla of British longboats attacked and captured a group of U.S. gunboats on Lake Borgne, next to Lake Ponchartrain just east of the city. The British were an easy march from New Orleans.

RIGHT MAN, RIGHT TIME, ROUGH PLACE

But bringing order from chaos was the willful Jackson. A battle-tested commander, "Old Hickory" had—with the help of frontiersman Davy Crockett and future president of the Republic of Texas Sam Houston—defeated a large uprising of Creek Indians in Mississippi Territory (today's Alabama) nine months before.

Jackson added to his troops' strength by recruiting pirates headed by French privateer Jean Lafitte, who for years had been seizing U.S. ships and smuggling contraband out of New Orleans. Just three months before, off the coast of southern Louisiana, a small American fleet had defeated one of Lafitte's. But the pirate leader reckoned the smuggling would be better under the Americans than the Brits. Jackson, despite terming the privateers "hellish banditti," needed fighters, so he pledged Lafitte and his men pardons if they fought for his side.

Gen. Jackson soon seized the initiative, attacking the British on December 23. The resulting skirmish was a draw, but the surprise assault gave the British pause, and bought the Americans time. On a bottleneck of land leading to New Orleans, Jackson's army built a tall, thousand-yard-long earthwork facing a shallow canal, which was anchored by an impassable swamp on one end and the Mississippi River to its west.

Into the Valley of Death

On January 8, 1815, the confident British attacked, with one column along the Mississippi, and the other against the breastworks. Along the river, a dam collapsed, delaying the planned assault past dawn. The attack seized a redoubt near the earthworks, but with a bayonet charge the U.S. 7th Infantry took it back.

The British were also slow to make their frontal assault on the ramparts, and thus attacked in broad daylight, their bright red coats supplying inviting targets. From on high, the Americans poured musket, rifle, grapeshot, and cannon fire, the latter from 32-pound guns to 6-inch howitzers. Recalled one American soldier: "Our men did not seem to apprehend any danger, but would load and fire as fast as they could, talking, swearing, and joking all the time."

On reaching the rampart, the British looked around for assault ladders—but an officer had forgotten them. Gen. Pakenham and his second-in-command were both shot dead off their horses. The remaining attackers halted, crawled, desperately looked for cover. An American officer cried out: "Shoot low, boys! shoot low! rake them—rake them! They're comin' on their all fours!"

By late morning, the battered British withdrew. A U.S. soldier observed that the "ground, extending from the ditch of our lines to that on which the enemy drew up his troops, 250 yards in length by about 200 in breadth, was literally covered with men, either dead or severely wounded." The casualty toll revealed one of the most lopsided significant battles in world history. The British suffered 484 captured or missing, 291 killed, and 1,267 wounded, in all, 2,042 casualties. The Americans, in contrast: 71 casualties, including 13 dead.

Ironically, the Battle of New Orleans took place two weeks after the Treaty of Ghent formally ended hostilities between Britain and America. In those pre-telegraph and pre-Internet days, word of the treaty traveled slowly.

News of the battle electrified a country seemingly poised for defeat. Jackson, a national hero, went on to win the presidency in 1828. The U.S. went on to retain Louisiana, and in time, gained much of the rest of western North America.

The Wright Brothers:
First to Fly

One hundred feet over the ground, the propeller shattered, and the primitive aircraft plummeted to earth. A passenger cracked opened his skull, and died—the first death from a plane crash. The pilot of this 1908 flight, Orville Wright, broke a leg, fractured and dislocated a hip, and shattered four ribs. In the hospital, a friend asked, "Has it got your nerve?" Orville—who with his brother Wilbur had made the first manned flight, and was now setting one aerial mark after another with test flights—was resolute:

"The only thing I'm afraid of is that I can't get well soon enough to finish those tests!"

The Dayton, Ohio brothers got right back on course. Within weeks, Orville had exceeded his own record of an hour-long continuous flight. The following autumn, Wilbur Wright flew around the Statue of Liberty and banked along the Hudson River, to the cheers of one million assembled New Yorkers. Their dazzling success resulted from years of patient, trial-and-error engineering.

FROM BICYCLES TO GLIDERS

Born in 1867 and 1871, respectively, Wilbur and Orville Wright first became fascinated with aviation as children, when their father brought home a toy—a rubber-band–driven helicopter. They immediately set about building one of their own.

As grown-ups, these inveterate tinkerers founded a firm to build, sell, and fix bicycles, one of the new inventions, along with motorcycles and cars, common in the thriving industrial center of Dayton. They indulged their love of flight, reading everything they could find on the glider flights of aviator Otto Lilienthal, and on the failed powered-flight attempts of Smithsonian director Samuel Langley.

To master the art of flying, they built and flew their own gliders. To improve the gliders, they invented the wind tunnel. They placed small airfoils to mimic wings on three-wheeled bikes that they comically pedaled about Dayton's streets. Then they took their experiments indoors, forcing air over a six-foot wooden airfoil, measuring the results of some 200 experiments with gear fashioned from saws and bicycle wire. Their wind tunnels were vastly more efficient and less costly than building a new glider for each test. And each test added to the brothers' growing knowledge of aerodynamics.

MAKING HISTORY AT KITTY HAWK

The brothers took their gliders to the windy, coastal bluffs of Kitty Hawk, North Carolina. There they became expert flyers. In

1902, they made 250 short glides in two days, and more than 1,000 in a month.

A simple purchase at the Wright Bike Company sparked another innovation. Wilbur was selling a customer an inner tube, and idly twisting the box. He was struck by the idea one could control a plane's flight in similar fashion, by twisting or "warping" its wings. The brothers successfully tested the notion on a five-foot kite, then applied it to their gliders, and finally to the plane they were building. The Wrights also discovered a pilot should "roll" or bank into the turn, like a bird, and unlike a ship, which is turned by a rudder. Their approach to flight borrowed much from cycling, where an inherently unstable rider on two thin tires stays upright by making constant adjustments.

By late 1903, the brothers had built and were eager to test their single-engine biplane. It was fashioned of strong, lightweight spruce, weighing a bit over 600 pounds, with a wingspan of 40 feet. Their bike mechanic, Charlie Taylor, built the 12-horsepower, gasoline-powered engine. Their twin, counter-rotating propellers, slung with bicycle-style drive chains, were almost as efficient as the wooden propellers of twenty-first-century airplanes. Astonishingly, in 1903 dollars, four years of designing, testing, and building cost the Wrights less than $1,000. An aviation historian termed their work the "most crucial and fruitful aeronautical experiments ever conducted in so short a time with so few materials and at so little expense."

The morning of December 17, 1903, was bitterly cold, with a 27-mph headwind at Kill Devil Hill near Kitty Hawk. Orville laid chest-down on the open-air plane, grasping the controls. He released the restraint, and the plane fought the wind to gain a height of ten feet, and traveled 120 feet before touching ground. Three more flights ensued, with the fourth lasting 59 seconds, and the distance leapfrogging to 852 feet. Then gusts rolled the craft over, damaging it, and ending the historic day. Yet the Wrights had made the first pilot-controlled, engine-powered, heavier-than-air flight in history.

Five years later came the triumphant flight over New York harbor. Sixty-one years after that, during the first Apollo mission to the moon, in 1969, astronaut Neil Armstrong honored his airborne predecessors by bringing along bits of wood and cloth from the 1903 Wright Flyer.

XI Corps and General Thomas Jonathan "Stonewall" Jackson: Defeat by the Master of Stealth and Surprise

The 11,000 men of the Union Army's XI Corps, at ease in the open field miles behind the front lines near Chancellorsville, Virginia on May 2, 1863, were starting to become uneasy. Late that afternoon, scores of animals and birds had started to pour out of the forest to their west, as if impelled forward by a terrible predator. Suddenly, a bloodcurdling cry from thousands of advancing Confederate soldiers issued from the woods, followed by a ferocious charge. Thousands of unprepared Union troops quickly surrendered or were put to flight. The remnants of the army gave up their effort to capture the Confederate capital of Richmond.

"Always mystify, mislead, and surprise the enemy," wrote Confederate Gen. Thomas Jonathan "Stonewall" Jackson, the man in charge of the daring flank assault. "Never fight against heavy odds, if by any possible maneuvering you can hurl your own force on only a part, and that the weakest part, of your enemy, and crush it."

AN ORPHAN SOLDIER

For one hailed by some as the greatest of American soldiers, Jackson had a unique and difficult background. His Protestant Scotch-Irish grandparents had been shipped from Londonderry to the American colonies in 1749 as indentured servants, after their conviction for larceny. During the American Revolution, his grandfather, John Jackson, fought in many bloody battles, rising to be a U.S. Army captain.

When Thomas Jackson was six, his mother died of complications during childbirth. Four years prior, his father and an elder sister had died of typhoid fever. Jackson and his surviving sister, Laura Ann, spent the rest of their childhood shuttling among relatives in western Virginia. When the Civil War came, Jackson would become estranged from his sister, a fierce proponent of the Union. Jackson's first wife, Ellie, would die in childbirth, after giving birth to a stillborn son. His first child from his second marriage, to Mary Anna Morrison, died soon after birth.

Lacking much formal education, the young Jackson would at night pore over books illuminated by lit pine knots. A slave gave him the knots in exchange for reading lessons, contrary to existing laws forbidding teaching a slave the alphabet. In 1842, Jackson's studious labors got him accepted to West Point. At first one of the most poorly prepared students, he ended up graduating 17th of 59 students in his class, again by staying up late studying, by the glow of coal embers, long after his fellow students had gone to bed.

Appointed second lieutenant of artillery, his first military action came in 1848 during the Mexican-American War. In the American assault on Mexico City's Chapultepec Castle, he refused a superior's "bad order" to withdraw, leading to a major American breakthrough. By war's end, U.S. Army chief Gen. Winfield Scott hailed Major Jackson as the most promoted American officer of the conflict.

From 1851 to 1861, Jackson served at the Virginia Military Institute (VMI) as a Professor of Natural and Experimental Philosophy—physics—and as Instructor of Artillery. He was a weak teacher, delivering rote lectures to the students, whom he punished if they asked for further explanation. The students responded by mocking him as "Fool Tom" and "Old Jack." In 1856, some alumni tried stripping Jackson of his professorship.

The future Confederate proved more popular among the area's slave and free black population. He and wife Mary Anna, fiercely devout, taught Sunday school at the local African-American Baptist church. Years later, when a grand equestrian statue of Jackson was commissioned in Richmond, the congregation was the first to contribute to its construction. Jackson and his wife owned six slaves, who during the Civil War were hired out or sold.

MASTER OF THE SUDDEN STRIKE

Prof. Jackson's stock swiftly rose with the outbreak of war. In July 1861, at Virginia's Bull Run, the Civil War's first major battle, his brigade broke the back of a surging Union attack, sending the Northern forces scurrying back to Washington, D.C. While Jackson had mustered his troops, the commander of a nearby unit, Gen. Barnard Bee, had shouted, "There is Jackson standing like a stone wall. Let us rally around the Virginians!" The nickname of Stonewall stuck to the laconic, resolute officer.

In spring 1862 Jackson achieved national renown with the

Shenandoah Valley campaign. He and his "Stonewall Brigade" of 17,000 men, although outnumbered more than 3 to 1, ejected three Union armies from the fertile valley, the Confederacy's "breadbasket." His swift-moving "foot cavalry" of infantrymen marched some 646 miles in 48 days, appearing out of nowhere to defeat one surprised Union force after another.

By now promoted to major general, Jackson became a key subordinate for the commander of the Army of Northern Virginia, Gen. Robert E. Lee. In this capacity, Jackson dealt the U.S. Army its greatest defeat ever, in terms of friendly-to-hostile casualties. In September 1862, at Harpers Ferry, Virginia, in modern-day West Virginia, Jackson's corps captured the Union garrison of 12,400 troops, losing only 39 of its own soldiers. He then quick-marched his men 15 miles to blood-stained Antietam, Maryland, where he and Lee barely halted the superior forces of Union Gen. George McClellan, with the two armies suffering 22,000 dead and wounded.

Eccentricities, and Deadly Daring

During this time, as his reputation grew, Stonewall's many eccentricities were noted. Convinced his left arm weighed less than his right, Jackson would keep it raised, so that "the blood might run back into his body and lighten it." The fearsome general was a poor rider, his stirrups far too short, which pulled his knees up to the level of his horse's back. His attire was that of an impoverished foot soldier, with a faded shirt, the buttons stripped off by admiring belles, a cap pulled down over piercing eyes.

His death in battle was a body blow to the Confederacy, which never again matched his successes. After scattering the Union right wing at Chancellorsville, Jackson had personally scouted out enemy positions that evening for a risky follow-up attack at night. On returning to the rebel lines, elements of a North Carolina regiment mistook him and his aides for Union cavalry, and opened fire. Three .57 caliber musket balls pierced Jackson's hand and left arm.

A surgeon amputated the arm, but Jackson died of pneumonia eight days after the battle. Just before expiring, he shouted deliriously, "Order [Gen.] A. P. Hill to prepare for action! Pass the infantry to the front rapidly!" Then he stated calmly, "Let us cross over the river, and rest under the shade of the trees." Upon Jackson's death, Lee noted: "[He] has lost his left arm but I my right."

But Jackson's martial influence lived on. In the twentieth century, his grandson became a U.S. general of artillery, his great-grandson a heroic pilot who died over Nazi-occupied France. Military academies around the world study his tactics.

In 1991, during the First Persian Gulf War, Saddam Hussein's Iraqi army occupying Kuwait was astonished when U.S.-led troops did not attack them head on. Instead, the U.S. commander, Gen. Norman Schwarzkopf, took a page out of Stonewall's playbook. He directed his speedy "armored cavalry" through the empty desert around the Iraqis' right wing, cutting off the main force. The ground war ended in six days.

THE BATTLE OF YORKTOWN:
THE WORLD TURNED UPSIDE DOWN

The bloody six-year war for independence had had its ups and downs for the U.S., but lately mostly downs. In the summer of 1781, the main American army, under Gen. George Washington, was encamped outside New York City, unable to dislodge the British army under Gen. Henry Clinton that was occupying the town. British units under Gen. Charles Lord Cornwallis and the traitorous Gen. Benedict Arnold had ravaged the South, marauding through the Carolinas and Virginia, before finally being forced to withdraw to the river port of Yorktown.

Therein lay an opportunity for the U.S., for in 1778, after patient diplomacy in Paris by diplomat Benjamin Franklin, the mighty French Empire had taken the rebels' side. Now the French had sent to America a powerful fleet of ships and soldiers under Admiral Comte de Grasse. Outside New York, the commanding French general Comte de Rochambeau met with Washington, and they agreed upon a bold gamble.

STEALING A MARCH

Leaving a small force to watch the British in New York City, their combined army began in mid-August to quickly march the 400 miles of trails and unpaved roads to Yorktown. The secretive advance was organized by Washington's second-in-command, Gen. Benjamin Lincoln. The Americans gulled Clinton with bogus messages indicating an imminent attack on New York City.

When the troops reached Philadelphia, crowds cheered, but the soldiers rebelled, demanding four weeks of back pay from the stingy Continental Congress there. Congress agreed. Meantime, Admiral De Grasse defeated a British fleet off the Virginia coast, hemming in Cornwallis from the sea. French transports then helped the Franco-American army on its journey southward.

Cornwallis got more nasty news in late September, when Washington and Rochambeau suddenly appeared outside his Yorktown encampment. Cornwallis' men and their German Hessian allies, their backs to a hostile sea, had about 9,000 troops, and meager stores of food. The French had 7,800 professional soldiers, the Americans 8,000 troops and 3,000 militia, including many German-Americans, and relatively plentiful supplies.

At Yorktown the Allies, through arduous labor, dug out 2,000 yards of siege trenches that paralleled the British lines. Then they began continuous cannonades that inflicted hundreds of casualties on the British and robbed them of rest. Next, in a nighttime assault, troops led by French nobleman Marquis de Lafayette and American Col. Alexander Hamilton, the future Treasury Secretary, seized two enemy redoubts. This let the Allies build another line of trenches even closer to the British. The Allied bombardments became more accurate and deadly. Cornwallis' men began to desert.

Cornwallis slaughtered hundreds of horses to feed his famished men, who also suffered from tidewater malaria. He sent a desperate letter to Gen. Clinton seeking reinforcements, but De Grasse's control of the sea made this request moot. The British tried a desperate breakout across the York River, but the Americans threw them back.

And the First Shall Be the Last

The enemy command realized its choices had run out. Cornwallis sent out a drummer boy and an officer with a white handkerchief of truce. Spotting the symbol of surrender, the Americans burst into raucous cheers, until they were silenced by Washington, who stated: "Let history huzzah for you."

On October 19, 1781, the British army threw in the towel. With Cornwallis absent, claiming to be ill, his defeated men marched between twin columns of French and American troops, the former resplendent in dress uniform, the latter ragged yet proud. Thousands of civilians watched in astonishment. The British were sullen, some trying to spike the weapons they handed over. The booty was impressive: 8,007 British and Hessian troops, over 200 cannon, thousands of muskets, and 24 ships.

The vanquished army's marching band caught the meaning of the day—that American independence was assured, having against unthinkable odds beaten the world's strongest military, despite having over eight years of war lost 25,000 men, of a population of 2.5 million. The musicians played a popular song befitting the outcome of the battle: "The World Turned Upside Down."

Two years later, the Treaty of Paris made it official: America was a new and sovereign nation.

THE ZENGER TRIAL:
FREEDOM OF EXPRESSION

The new governor of the royal colony of New York, William Cosby, wasn't winning many friends. He demanded half the salary of his predecessor, Rip Van Dam, an esteemed, 71-year-old provincial council member. Van Dam had served as acting governor for a year until Cosby assumed power in 1731. When Van Dam refused to turn over the money, New York's Supreme Court ruled against him, despite the dissenting vote of Chief Justice Lewis Morris. Cosby then had Morris sacked, and replaced him with loyalist judge James DeLancey. When Morris ran for assemblyman, Cosby disallowed the ballots of pro-Morris Quakers. The grudge-holding governor also appointed a crony the censor of the colony's sole newspaper, the *New York Gazette*.

THE SPROUTS OF DEMOCRACY

Morris, Van Dam, and a prominent New York lawyer, James Alexander, refused to buckle. They formed an opposition group, the Popular Party. In addition, Alexander founded the country's first independent newspaper, the *New York Weekly Journal,* printed by a German immigrant, John Peter Zenger. Each Monday, Zenger published an anonymous weekly column of Alexander's that lambasted Cosby's arrogant and grasping rule. "No nation ancient or modern," wrote Alexander, "has ever lost the liberty of freely speaking, writing or publishing their sentiments, but forthwith lost their liberty in general and became slaves."

Gov. Cosby was enraged at the paper's "libel," as any critique of authority was then deemed. He demanded that the colonial Assembly burn the *Journal* in public, but the assemblymen refused. In January 1734, Chief Justice DeLancey requested that a grand jury indict the *Journal*'s operators on sedition and libel, but the grand jury declined. In October, DeLancey asked the same of another grand jury, which slyly asserted it couldn't identify the author of the anonymous attacks.

Finally, Cosby got DeLancey and a second compliant judge to issue a warrant for the arrest of Zenger. In November the publisher was hauled into jail, and saddled with an enormous £800 bail bond.

The warrant accused Zenger of "printing and publishing several seditious libels . . . having in them many things tending to raise factions and tumults among the people of this Province, inflaming their minds with contempt of His Majesty's government, and greatly disturbing the peace." Zenger refused to be cowed. Communicating with his wife through a hole in the prison door, he issued instructions to keep the *Journal* in circulation. The newspaper published his jailhouse letters, which gained much public sympathy.

HIRING A PHILADELPHIA LAWYER

With Zenger's trial looming, the obvious lawyer to defend him was Alexander—but Gov. Cosby had him disbarred. So Alexander, with help from Philadelphia printer Benjamin Franklin, persuaded the colonies' most eloquent lawyer, Philadelphia's James Hamilton, to take up the case, *pro bono*. Alexander helped prepare Hamilton's legal brief.

Cosby tried stacking the jury, filling the list of potential jurors with "non-freeholders," men who managed landed estates at the governor's whim. But even Cosby's handpicked Judge DeLancey thought this tactic heavy-handed, and seated a normal jury of twelve of Zenger's peers. (In happier times, Judge DeLancey chartered what became New York's Columbia University; Manhattan's Delancey Street is named for him.)

Presided over by bewigged, red-robed judges, the trial began at City Hall on August 4, 1734. Attorney General Richard Bradley kicked things off by accusing Zenger of being a "frequent printer and publisher of false news and seditious libels." Defense attorney Hamilton then shocked the courtroom by admitting that Zenger had printed the supposedly libelous articles. Hamilton argued that Zenger was still innocent, however, because the opinions he published, though critical of authority, were true. When a governing authority like Cosby overstepped his bounds, the attorney reasoned, a citizen had a right and a duty to call him out. Hamilton advocated an early version of "jury nullification," by which jurors can acquit a defendant who violates a law that is unjust or misapplied.

Hamilton pleaded: "Power may justly be compared to a great river. While kept within its due bounds it is both beautiful and useful. But when it overflows its banks, it is then too impetuous to be stemmed; it bears down all before it, and brings destruction and desolation wherever it comes." The attorney concluded: "Nature and the laws of our country have given us a right to liberty of both exposing and opposing arbitrary power by speaking and writing truth."

On August 5, the jury withdrew to deliberate. It soon reentered the packed courtroom. Foreman Thomas Hunt read the verdict: "Not guilty." The court exploded in cheers. An irate Chief Justice DeLancey threatened the celebrants with jail, to no avail.

FREEDOM FOR PRISONER, FREEDOM OF SPEECH

Zenger was released. The city set off cannonades in honor of Hamilton, for whom the term "Philadelphia lawyer," with its original meaning of skillful attorney, was coined. New York's Common Council presented him with a gold box inscribed with words from Cicero: "For let the laws be never so much overborne by some one individual's power, let the spirit of freedom be never so intimidated, still sooner or later they assert themselves."

Partly due to the Zenger case, a notion took hold in the colonies that the press should be allowed to freely criticize the ruling authorities. This idea took full blossom in the American Revolution, when pamphlets like Thomas Paine's *Common Sense* called for replacing an overweening king with a democratic republic. The Zenger case also led to the guarantees of freedom of the press and freedom of speech stated in the First Amendment to the Constitution.

Indeed, it was the great-grandson of Zenger ally Lewis Morris, New York's Gouverneur Morris, who wrote the Constitution's "We the People" preamble. Gouverneur Morris also wrote: "The trial of Zenger was the germ of American freedom, the morning star of that liberty which subsequently revolutionized America."

BIBLIOGRAPHY

About North Georgia. "Sequoyah (a.k.a. George Gist)." Last modified
2011. http://ngeorgia.com/ang/Sequoyah(a.k.a_George_Gist).

———. "The Trail of Tears." Last modified 1997. http://ngeorgia.
com/history/nghisttt.html.

Adams, John. *The Works of John Adams, Vol. II, The Diary*, 1850.
Edited by Charles Francis Adams. Reprinted in Maier Pauline,
American Scripture: Making the Declaration of Independence. New
York: Vintage, 1997.

Agronsky, Jonathan. "Charles Augustus Lindbergh." U.S. Centennial
of Flight Commission, 2003. http://www.centennialofflight.gov/essay/
Explorers_Record_Setters_and_Daredevils/Lindbergh/EX15.htm.

"Alexander Graham Bell." Smithsonian, National Museum of American History. http://invention.smithsonian.org/centerpieces/iap/inventors_bel.html.

Alexander Hamilton. PBS, 1997.

Ambrose, Stephen. *Undaunted Courage: Meriwether Lewis, Thomas Jefferson, and the Opening of the American West.* New York: Simon & Schuster, 1997.

American Business Hall of Fame. "Cyrus McCormick, International Harvester Company." http://www.anbhf.org/laureates/mccormick.html.

AmericanCivilWar.com. "Clara Barton, 1821-1912, Civil War Nurse, Founder American Red Cross." http://americancivilwar.com/women/cb.html.

American Red Cross Museum. *A Brief History of the American Red Cross.* http://www.redcross.org/museum/history/brief.asp.

AmericanRhetoric. Martin Luther King, Jr. *"I Have a Dream."* Delivered 28 August 1963. Estate of Dr. Martin Luther King, Jr. http://www.americanrhetoric.com/speeches/mlkihaveadream.htm.

Antonelli, Kathleen R. "John Mauchly's Early Years." *Annals of the History of Computing* 6 (2).

Arlington National Cemetery. "Visitor Information." http://www.arlingtoncemetery.mil/visitor_information/index.htm.

AtomicArchive.com. "The Manhattan Project: Making the Atomic Bomb." National Science Digital Library. Last modified 2011. http://www.atomicarchive.com/History/mp/index.shtml.

Aveni, Anthony. "The Indian Origins of Lacrosse." *Colonial Williamsburg Journal* (Winter 2010).

Barton, Clara. *The Red Cross-In Peace and War*. Washington, D.C.: American Historical Press, 1898.

"The Battle of New Orleans." *The Louisiana Historical Quarterly* IX, no. 1 (January 1926).

BBC. "The Origins of Yellowstone National Park, USA." http://www.bbc.co.uk/dna/h2g2/A3577197.

Beveridge, Charles E. "Frederick Law Olmsted Sr." National Association for Olmsted Parks. In *Pioneers of American Landscape Design*, edited by Birnbaum, Charles A., FASLA, and Robin Karson. New York: McGraw-Hill Companies, 2000. http://www.olmsted.org/the-olmsted-legacy/frederick-law-olmsted-sr.

Beveridge, Charles E., and Paul Rocheleau. *Frederick Law Olmsted: Designing the American Landscape*. New York: Rizzoli International, 1995.

Bloom, Sol. "The Story of the Constitution." Washington, D.C.: National Archives and Record Administration, 1986.

Borneman, Walter R. *Polk: The Man Who Transformed the Presidency and America*. New York: Random House, 2008.

Bradford, William, *Of Plymouth Plantation 1620-1647*. New York: Random House, 1981.

Braunwart, Bob, and Bob Carroll. *The Journey to Camp: The Origins of American Football from Ancient Times to 1889*. The Professional Football Researchers Association.

Bruno, Leonard C. "The Invention of the Telegraph." The Library of Congress, Manuscript Division.

Bruns, Roger A. "A More Perfect Union: The Creation of the United States Constitution." Washington, D.C.: National Archives and Records Administration by the National Archives Trust Fund Board, 1986.

Buckman, David. *Old Steamboat Days on the Hudson River*. New York: The Grafton Press, 1907.

Burns, Ken. *Lewis & Clark: The Journey of the Corps of Discovery*. Washington, D.C.: WETA/PBS, 1997.

Case, Steven. "James Knox Polk." NCPedia. Last modified September 11, 2009. http://ncpedia.org/biography/polk-james.

Centers for Disease Control and Prevention (CDC). "The Panama Canal." Last modified February 8, 2010. http://www.cdc.gov/malaria/about/history/panama_canal.html.

Chantrill, Christopher. USGovernmentSpending.com.

Chernow, Ron. *Alexander Hamilton*. New York: Penguin Press, 2004.

————. *Titan: The Life of John D. Rockefeller, Sr.* New York: Vintage, 2004.

The Civil War, Vol. 5. Compiled and edited by Time-Life Books. New York: Time Inc., 1984.

Clark University, Archives and Special Collections. "Dr. Robert H. Goddard, Frequently Asked Questions." http://www.clarku.edu/research/archives/goddard/faqs.cfm.

Collins, Glenn. "Politics and Sacred Ground, 1853; Birth of Central Park Holds Parallels With Ground Zero." The *New York Times*, May 15, 2003.

Columbia College Chicago, Archives. "William LeBaron Jenney." http://www.lib.colum.edu/archives/college/buildings/lejenney.htm.

Crouch, Tom. "The Unlikely Inventors." *NOVA*. PBS, November 11, 2003.

Crouch, Tom, and Peter L. Jakab. *The Wright Brothers and the Invention of the Aerial Age.* Washington, D.C.: National Geographic, 2003.

De la Cova, Dr. Antonio Rafael. "Brief History of the Panama Canal." Latin American Studies.org. Last modified 1997. http://www.latinamericanstudies/canal/canal-history.htm.

Department of the Interior, Bureau of Land Management. "History of the Transcontinental Railroad." Last modified March 4, 2011. http://www.blm.gov/ut/st/en/fo/salt_lake/recreation/back_country_byways/transcontinental_railroad/transcontinental_railroad.html.

Dobbs, Michael. *One Minute to Midnight: Kennedy, Khrushchev, and Castro on the Brink of Nuclear War*. New York: Alfred A. Knopf, 2008.

Douglass, Frederick. *Life and Times of Frederick Douglass*. 1881, revised 1892.

———. *A Narrative of the Life of Frederick Douglass, an American Slave*. 1845.

Easterbrook, Gregg. "Forgotten Benefactor of Humanity." *The Atlantic*, 1997.

Ehle, John. *Trail of Tears: The Rise and Fall of the Cherokee Nation*. New York: Doubleday, 1988.

"Ellis Island." The Statue of Liberty-Ellis Island Foundation, Inc. Last modified 2010. http://www.ellisisland.org/genealogy/ellis_island.asp.

Ellis, Joseph J. *Founding Brothers: The Revolutionary Generation*. New York: Vintage, 2002.

The Eniac. Last modified December 2010. http://the-eniac.com/people-machines-and-politics-of-the-cyber-age-creation/.

EyeWitness to History. "The Battle of New Orleans, 1815." Last modified 2006. http://www.eyewitnesstohistory.com/battleofneworleans.htm.

———. "Completing the Transcontinental Railroad, 1869." Last modified 2004. http://www.eyewitnesstohistory.com/goldenspike.htm.

———. "Writing the Declaration of Independence, 1776." Last modified 1999. http://www.eyewitnesstohistory.com/jefferson.htm.

Fenster, Julie M. "Inventing the Telephone—And Triggering All-Out Patent War." *American Heritage*, March 7, 2006.

"Flight 93 hijacker: 'Shall we finish it off?'" CNN.com, July 23, 2004. http://www.cnn.com/2004/US/07/22/911.flight.93/.

Ford, Henry, and Samuel Crowther. *My Life and Work*. New York: Doubleday, 1922.

Franklin, Benjamin. *The Autobiography of Benjamin Franklin*.

Freeman, Douglas S. *R. E. Lee, A Biography*. New York: Scribners, 1934.

Frith, Holden. "Major William Le Baron Jenney" (Skyscrapers). *The Sunday Times* (London), February 7, 2005.

Gabler, Neal. *Walt Disney: The Triumph of the American Imagination*. New York: Knopf, 2006.

Goodwin, Joan. "Clara Barton." Unitarian Universalist Historical Society. Last modified 2011. http://www25.uua.org/uuhs/duub/articles/clarabarton.html.

Gordon, John Steele. "A Short History of the National Debt." *Wall Street Journal*, February 8, 2009.

Gorgas, W. C. "Malaria prevention on the Isthmus of Panama." *The Prevention of Malaria*, by Ross, R. New York: E. P. Dutton & Co., 1910.

Gosling, F. G. *The Manhattan Project: Making the Atomic Bomb*. Department of Energy, January 1999.

Gross, Daniel. *Greatest Business Stories of All Time*. New York: John Wiley & Sons, 1997.

Historical Society of the Courts of the State of New York. "A Brief Narrative of the Case and Tryal of John Peter Zenger." 1736.

Hudson River Maritime Museum. "Robert Fulton, the Clermont and Other Early Steamboats." http://www.hrmm.org/Robert_Fulton/robert_fulton.html.

Hutchinson, W. T. *Cyrus Hall McCormick*. New York: Da Capo Press, 1968.

IMDb, The Internet Movie Database. "Walt Disney." Last modified 2011. http://www.imdb.com/name/nm0000370/.

"Inside the Corps." From *Lewis and Clark: The Journey of the Corps of Discovery (A Film by Ken Burns)*. Florentine Films and WETA/PBS Online. http://www.pbs.org/lewisandclark/inside/index.html.

Inventors Hall of Fame. "Alexander Graham Bell." Last modified 2007. http://www.invent.org/hall_of_fame/11.html.

Jacobs, Jane. *Life and Death of the Great American City*. Cambridge, MA: M.I.T. Press, 1961.

Jenkins, Reese V. et al., eds. *The Papers of Thomas A. Edison: The Making of an Inventor, February 1847 - June 1873*. Baltimore: Johns Hopkins University Press, 1989.

"John Marshall." Exhibit, 2001. The Library of Virginia. Last modified 2001. http://www.lva.virginia.gov/exhibits/marshall/.

"John W. Mauchly and the Development of the ENIAC Computer." University of Pennsylvania, Penn Libraries Exhibitions. Last modified February 3, 2003.

Johnson, Paul. *History of the American People*. New York: Harper Perennial, 1999.

Johnson, Robert Underwood, and Clarence Clough Buell. *Battles and Leaders of the Civil War: Volume 2*. Castle Books, 1985.

Keller, Helen. *The Story of My Life*. New York: Doubleday, Page & Company, 1903.

Kelly, Fred C. *Miracle at Kitty Hawk: The Letters of Wilbur and Orville Wright*. New York: Farrar, Straus, and Young, 1951.

Kluger, Jeffrey. "Rocket Scientist Robert Goddard." *Time*, March 29, 1999.

Kodak. "George Eastman." http://www.kodak.com/global/en/corp/historyOfKodak/eastmanTheMan.jhtml?pq-path=2689&pq-locale=en_US.

The Lemelson Center for the Study of Invention & Innovation. "Edison's Story." http://invention.smithsonian.org/centerpieces/edison/000_story_02.asp.

Lewis, Meriwether, and William Clark. *The Journals of Lewis and Clark, 1804-1806*. Reprint of the 1904-1906 editions, Project Gutenberg, 2005. http://www.gutenberg.org/ebooks/8419.

Library of Congress, American Memory. "The Life of Thomas A. Edison." http://memory.loc.gov/ammem/edhtml/edbio.html.

———. "Girard's Bank."

Lindbergh, Charles A. *The Spirit of St. Louis*. New York: Charles Scribner's Sons, 1953.

———. *WE*. New York & London: G. P. Putnam's Sons, 1927.

Linder, Doug. "The Trial of John Peter Zenger and the Birth of Freedom of the Press." Washington, D.C.: U.S. Department of State, April 2008.

Lindsay, David. "People & Events: George Eastman." From *The Wizard of Photography*. WGBH / PBS Online. 2000. http://www.pbs.org/wgbh/amex/eastman/peopleevents/pande02.html.

Lord, Walter. *Incredible Victory: The Battle of Midway*. Ithaca, NY: Burford Books, 1998.

Lowry, Rich. "The People's Tycoon: Driven." *The New York Times*, September 4, 2005.

Malone, Dumas. *Jefferson and His Time*. Charlottesville, VA: University of Virginia Press, 2005.

Marconi, Elaine M. "Robert Goddard: A Man and His Rocket." NASA Missions. Last modified March 9, 2004. http://www.nasa.gov/missions/research/f_goddard.html.

McCullough, David. *John Adams*. New York: Simon & Schuster, 2001.

————. "Lindbergh." Enhanced Transcript. Insignia Films Production for The American Experience WGBH Educational Foundation Thirteen/WNET and Insignia Films / PBS, 1990. http://www.pbs.org/wgbh/amex/lindbergh/filmmore/transcript/index.html.

————. *The Path Between the Seas: The Creation of the Panama Canal, 1870-1914.* New York: Simon & Schuster, 1978.

McDougall, Walter A. *Freedom Just Around the Corner: A New American History: 1585-1828.* New York: Harper Perennial, 2005.

McManus, John C. "Spirit of New Orleans." Last modified April 29, 2008. http://www.historynet.com/spirit-of-new-orleans.htm.

Merry, Robert W. *A Country of Vast Designs: James K. Polk, the Mexican War and the Conquest of the American Continent.* New York: Simon & Schuster, 2009.

MIT. "Inventor of the Week: The Telephone." Last modified 2000. http://web.mit.edu/invent/iow/graham_bell.html.

Mitchell, John G. "Frederick Law Olmstead." *National Geographic* magazine, March 2005. http://ngm.nationalgeographic.com/ngm/0503/feature2/fulltext.html.

————. "Cyrus McCormick." Last modified 2000. http://web.mit.edu/invent/iow/mccormick.html.

Moore, Matthew. "Google marks Samuel Morse's birthday with code logo." *London Telegraph*, April 27, 2009. http://www.telegraph.co.uk/technology/google/5229160/Google-marks-Samuel-Morses-birthday-with-code-logo.html.

Moser, Edward P. *The Politically Correct Guide to American History.* New York: Crown Publishers/Random House, 1996.

Naismith Museum. "Biography of James Naismith." http://www. naismithmuseum.com/main.php?action=cms.JamesNaismith.

NASA, Centers. "Dr. Robert H. Goddard, American Rocketry Pioneer." Last modified August 14, 1999. http://www.nasa.gov/ centers/goddard/about/dr_goddard.html.

National Archives. "Declaration of Independence." http://www. archives.gov/exhibits/charters/declaration.html.

———. "Louisiana Purchase." http://www.archives.gov/exhibits/ american_originals_iv/sections/text_purchase_treaty.html.

National Commission on Terrorist Attacks Upon the United States. *9/11 Commission Report.* New York: W. W. Norton & Company, 2004.

"The National Parks: America's Best Idea (A Film by Ken Burns)." PBS, 2009. http://www.pbs.org/nationalparks/.

National Park Service, U.S. Department of the Interior. "Ellis Island." http://www.nps.gov/elis/historyculture/index.htm.

———. "Find a Park." http://www.nps.gov/findapark/index.htm.

———. "The Great Garrison Flag." http://www.nps.gov/archive/ fomc/tguide/Lesson8a.htm.

———. "John Marshall." http://www.nps.gov/history/nr/twhp/ wwwlps/lessons/49marshall/49facts1.htm.

————. "The Lewis and Clark Journey of Discovery." http://
www.nps.gov/archive/jeff/lewisclark2/circa1804/heritage/
LouisianaPurchase/LouisianaPurchase.htm.

————. "Statue of Liberty National Monument."

————. "The Trail of Tears and the Forced Relocation of the
Cherokee Nation." http://www.nps.gov/history/nr/twhp/wwwlps/
lessons/118trail/118trail.htm.

————. "Wright Brothers." http://www.nps.gov/wrbr/
historyculture/index.htm.

————. "Yellowstone National Park: Its Exploration and
Establishment." 2000.

Nevins, Allan, and Frank Ernest Hill. *Ford: The Times, the Man, the
Company*. New York: Scribners, 1954.

Nielsen, Kim E. *Beyond the Miracle Worker: The Remarkable Life of
Anne Sullivan Macy and Her Extraordinary Friendship with Helen
Keller*. Boston: Beacon Press, 2010.

Olmsted, Frederick Law. *The Cotton Kingdom: A Traveller's
Observations on Cotton and Slavery in the American Slave States.
Based Upon Three Former Volumes of Journeys and Investigations*.
New York: Mason Brothers, 1862.

Ozick, Cynthia. "What Helen Keller Saw." *The New Yorker*, June 16,
2003.

"The Panama Canal." Eclipse.com. http://www.eclipse.
co.uk/~sl5763/panama.htm#History.

Parshall, Jonathan, and Anthony Tully. *Shattered Sword: The Untold Story of the Battle of Midway.* Dulles, VA: Potomac Books, 2005.

"People & Discoveries: Jonas Salk: 1914-1995." From *A Science Odyssey.* WGBH / PBS Online. Last modified 1998.

"People & Events: Cyrus McCormick (1809-1884)." From *Chicago: City of the Century.* WGBH Boston / PBS Online. 2003. http://www. pbs.org/wgbh/amex/chicago/peopleevents/p_mccormick.html.

Poe, Edgar Allan. *Complete Stories and Poems of Edgar Allan Poe.* New York: Doubleday, 1984.

Poole, Keith. "People & Events: John D. Rockefeller Senior, 1839-1937." *The Rockefellers.* WGBH / PBS Online. 2000. http://www.pbs. org/wgbh/amex/rockefellers/peopleevents/p_rock_jsr.html.

Prange, Gordon. *At Dawn We Slept: The Untold Story of Pearl Harbor.* New York: Penguin, 1982.

Preservation Virginia. "The John Marshall House." http://www. preservationvirginia.org/marshall/justice/.

Prime, Samuel Iren Aeus. *The Life of Samuel F. B. Morse: Inventor of the Electro-Magnetic Telegraph.* New York: D. Appleton and Company, 1875.

Pryor, Elizabeth Brown. *Clara Barton: Professional Angel.* Philadelphia: University of Pennsylvania Press, 1987.

Quinn, Kenneth M. "Norman Borlaug." The World Food Prize, Full Biography. Last modified 2011. http://www.worldfoodprize.org/ index.cfm?nodeID=25305&audienceID=1.

Reid, T. R. "The Superhighway to Everywhere." *Washington Post,* June 28, 2006.

Remini, Robert V. *Andrew Jackson.* New York: Harper Perennial, 1999.

———. *The Battle of New Orleans: Andrew Jackson and America's First Military Victory.* New York: Penguin, 1999.

Rhodes, Richard. *The Making of the Atomic Bomb.* New York: Simon & Schuster, 1995.

"Robert Fulton and His Life's Work." *Scientific American,* September 25, 1909.

Robertson, James. *Stonewall Jackson.* New York: Macmillan, 1997.

Roddy, Dennis B. "Flight 93: Forty lives, one destiny." *Post-Gazette,* October 28, 2001.

Root, M. A. *The Camera and The Pencil: or the Heliographic Art.* Philadelphia: J. B. Lippincott & Co., 1864. From the Daguerreian Society, 1999, http://www.daguerre.org.

Ryan, Cornelius. *The Longest Day: The Classic Epic of D-Day.* New York: Simon & Schuster, 1994.

Schmeck Jr., Harold M. "Dr. Jonas Salk, Whose Vaccine Turned Tide on Polio, Dies at 80." *New York Times,* June 24, 1995.

Schmidt, Thomas. *National Geographic Guide to the Lewis & Clark Trail.* Washington, D.C.: National Geographic, 2002.

Segall, Grant. *John D. Rockefeller: Anointed With Oil.* New York: Oxford University Press, 2001.

Snyder, Logan Thomas. "President Dwight Eisenhower and America's Interstate Highway System." *American History*, June 2006.

"The Star Spangled Banner." Exhibit. Smithsonian, National Museum of American History. http://americanhistory.si.edu/starspangledbanner/.

"Statue of Liberty National Monument: History of Statue of Liberty." OhRanger.com. Last modified 2011. http://www.ohranger.com/statue-liberty/history-statue-liberty.

Thomas Jefferson Foundation. "The Louisiana Purchase." Monticello.org. http://www.monticello.org/site/jefferson/louisiana-purchase.

Thomas, Sandra. *Frederick Douglass, "Abolitionist/Editor": A Biography of the Life of Frederick Douglass.* University of Rochester, http://www.history.rochester.edu/class/douglass/HOME.html.

Thompson, Fred. "Henry Ford." *Fordism, Post-Fordism, and the Flexible System of Production.* From Willamette University Online. http://www.willamette.edu/~fthompso/MgmtCon/Henry_Ford.html.

Thorpe, Francis Newton, ed. "The Federal and State Constitutions Colonial Charters, and Other Organic Laws of the States, Territories, and Colonies Now or Heretofore Forming the United States of America." Compiled and edited under the Act of Congress of June 30, 1906. Government Printing Office: Washington, D.C.: 1909.

Thurston, Robert H. *Robert Fulton: His Life and its Results*. New York: Dodd, Mead, and Company Publishers, 1891.

Toponce, Alexander. *Alexander Toponce, Pioneer*. 1923.

"TR's Legacy - The Panama Canal." From *TR, the Story of Theodore Roosevelt*. The *American Experience* and WGBH Interactive / PBS Online. 1997. http://www.pbs.org/wgbh/amex/tr/panama.html.

"Transcontinental Railroad." HiddenHill Productions film and the *American Experience* / PBS Online. 2003. http://www.pbs.org/wgbh/amex/tcrr/index.html.

Trapp, Dan. "Jean Baptiste Charbonneau." *Encyclopedia of Frontier Biography Vol 1*. Lincoln, NE: University of Nebraska Press, 1988.

University of Missouri, St. Louis. "Louisiana Purchase Bicentennial." http://www.umsl.edu/~loupurch/history.html.

U.S. Department of Energy. *The Manhattan Project*. Last modified January 2010. http://energy.gov/sites/prod/files/edg/media/The_Manhattan_Project_2010.pdf.

U.S. Department of the Navy. "Oral History - Battle of Midway." Naval History & Heritage Command. Last modified May 11, 2009. http://www.history.navy.mil/faqs/faq81-8.htm.

———. "Oral History - Battle of Midway, Recollections of Lieutenant George Gay." Naval History & Heritage Command. Last modified February 15, 2001. http://www.history.navy.mil/faqs/faq81-8c.htm.

———. "Pearl Harbor Raid, 7 December 1941, Overview and Special Image Selection." U.S. Navy, Naval History & Heritage Command. http://www.history.navy.mil/photos/events/wwii-pac/pearlhbr/pearlhbr.htm.

U.S. Department of Transportation, Federal Highway Administration. "Dwight D. Eisenhower National System of Interstate and Defense Highways." Last modified April 7, 2011. http://www.fhwa.dot.gov/programadmin/interstate.cfm.

U.S. Supreme Court Center. "Marbury v. Madison (1803)." FindLaw.com. Last modified 2011. http://supreme.lp.findlaw.com/supreme_court/landmark/marbury.html.

Vermont Division for Historic Preservation. "Justin Smith Morrill Homestead." http://www.historicvermont.org/morrill/.

Washington, George. "1789 Thanksgiving Proclamation by George Washington." Papers at the Library of Congress.

Watterson, John S. "Inventing Modern Football." *American Heritage*, September/October 1988.

Wikipedia. "Nicholas Biddle," http://en.wikipedia.org/wiki/Nicholas_Biddle_(banker).

———. "Samuel Morse." Last modified September 30, 2011. http://en.wikipedia.org/wiki/Samuel_Morse.

Wilford, John Noble. "On Hand for Space History, as Superpowers Spar." The *New York Times*, July 13, 2009.

Williams, Juan. *Eyes on the Prize: America's Civil Rights Years, 1954-1965*. New York: Penguin, 1988.

Wills, Garry. *Inventing America: Jefferson's Declaration of Independence*. New York: Mariner Books, 2002.

Wilson, George. *Stephen Girard*. Conshohocken, PA: Combined Books, 1995.

Wilson, John S. "Benny Goodman, King of Swing, Is Dead." *The New York Times*, June 14, 1986.

Wong, Edward. "Baseball's Disputed Origin Is Traced Back, Back, Back." *The New York Times*, July 8, 2001.

"Wright Brothers History." U.S. Centennial of Flight Commission, 2003. http://www.centennialofflight.gov/wbh/index.htm.

Wu, Corinna. "Old Glory, New Glory, The Star-Spangled Banner gets some tender loving care." *Science News* 155 (26).